West Yorkshire Vol I
Edited by Steve Twelvetree

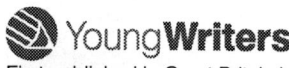

First published in Great Britain in 2004 by:
Young Writers
Remus House
Coltsfoot Drive
Peterborough
PE2 9JX
Telephone: 01733 890066
Website: www.youngwriters.co.uk

All Rights Reserved

© Copyright Contributors 2004

SB ISBN 1 84460 496 9

Foreword

Young Writers was established in 1991 and has been passionately devoted to the promotion of reading and writing in children and young adults ever since. The quest continues today. Young Writers remains as committed to engendering the fostering of burgeoning poetic and literary talent as ever.

This year's Young Writers competition has proven as vibrant and dynamic as ever and we are delighted to present a showcase of the best poetry from across the UK. Each poem has been carefully selected from a wealth of *Once Upon A Rhyme* entries before ultimately being published in this, our twelfth primary school poetry series.

Once again, we have been supremely impressed by the overall high quality of the entries we have received. The imagination, energy and creativity which has gone into each young writer's entry made choosing the best poems a challenging and often difficult but ultimately hugely rewarding task - the general high standard of the work submitted amply vindicating this opportunity to bring their poetry to a larger appreciative audience.

We sincerely hope you are pleased with our final selection and that you will enjoy *Once Upon A Rhyme West Yorkshire Vol I* for many years to come.

Contents

Ash Grove J&I School

Alexandra Horner (9)	1
Bethany Hammond (9)	1
Tyler Duke (9)	2
Danielle Thomas (9)	2
Jessica Tetlow (9)	3
Frazer Hawkins (9)	3
Kane Appleton (9)	4
Jared Armstrong (9)	4
Lewis Germain (9)	5
Christopher Pagdin (9)	5
Danny Vaquero (9)	6
Bethany Hirst (10)	6
Jon Downing (9)	7
Bradley Bateman (10)	7
Danielle Foulds (9)	8
Danielle Haigh (10)	8
Megan Hemingway (10)	9
Bradley Dwyer (9)	9
Daniel Ingham (10)	10
Andrew Mapston (10)	10
Curtis Cowell (9)	10
Sam Whitehouse (9)	11
Hannah Stoppard (10)	11
Melissa Cocliff (9)	12
Shannen Hall (10)	12
Ben Broad (9)	13
Caitlin Smaldon (10)	13
Jake Bench (10)	14
Roxanne Adamson (10)	14
Lewis Philips (10)	14
Heather Andrew (9)	15
Lewis Clark (10)	15
Ashley Daykin (10)	16
Michael Kirby (10)	16
Hayley Lockett (10)	17
Liam Rollin (10)	17
Jake Thomas (10)	18
Amy Evans (10)	18

Samuel Womersley (10)   19

Bramley St Peter's CE Primary School
Emily Benton (9)   19
Kimberley Carrick (9)   20
Katie Fahy (10)   21
Camille Reed (10)   21
Reece Harrison (9)   22
Dale Reece Oyston (9)   22
Ariane Daniels (9)   22
Gemma Louise Kennally (9)   23
Tanieka Kargwal (10)   24
Eleanor Davies (9)   24
Jake Nevison (10)   25
Hannah Fawcett (9)   25
Ted Thompson-Melling (9)   26
Joseph Pearson (10)   26
Christina Storey (9)   27
Aaran Whitehead (10)   27
Matthew Stitch (10)   28
Bryoni Alderson (10)   29

Brotherton and Byram CP School
Jamie Baxter (11)   29
Gemma Brooks (10)   30
Charlotte Heale (10)   30
Hannah Price (10)   31
Natalie Clough (10)   31
Laura Golding (11)   32
Autumn Newby (10)   32
Tanya Williamson (10)   33
Aquilla Berenice Softley (10)   33
Lauren Clisby (10)   33
Lauren Ramsey (10)   34
Devon Croft (11)   35
Jodie Tate (11)   36
Bradley Hunter (10)   36
Nicole Halliday (11)   37

Carlton Road J&I School
Thomas Farmer (8)	37
Joshua Mitchell (9)	38
Morgan Williams (8)	39
Kayleigh Varey (9)	39
Gary Curtis (10)	39
Imogen Copley (10)	40
Macauly Kolka (9)	40
Kelly Sheppard (10)	41
Rachel Burridge (9)	41
Ryan Lees (9)	41
Lee Sykes (9)	42
Joshua Green (9)	43
Dionne Dockerty Shields (10)	44
Jasmine Evans (9)	45
Jenna Leigh Butterfield (9)	46
Lauren Clements (9)	47
Kaysha Leiah Smith (9)	48
Victoria Jade Sheppard (10)	49
Dominic Yates (9)	50
Daniel Hugill (10)	51
Luke Malone (9)	52

Farsley Springbank Junior School
Amy Edgley (10)	52
Olivia Louise Platt (9)	53
Stephanie Lacey (9)	53
Megan Atack (10)	54
Christina Lang (9)	54
Amy Ann Sutcliffe (9)	54
Lucy Hall (9)	55
Megan Harrison (9)	55
Caitlin Louise McCafferty (10)	56
Bethany Shaw (9)	56
Richard Thomas Whitley-Peden (9)	56
Abby Coates (9)	57
Rebecca Donaldson (9)	57
Ryan Rogers (9)	57
Rachel Louise Rogers (9)	58
Nicole Bramley (10)	58
Karl Morris (9)	58

Adam Swales (9)	59
Bethany Grace Gaunt (10)	59
Lewis James Thornton (10)	59
Emma Jennings (10)	60
Megan Paige Reed (9)	60
Olivia Mary Taylor (10)	60
Bethany Broadbent (10)	61
Jamie Mark Kemp (9)	61
Joe Firth (10)	61
Joseph Pritchard (9)	62
Ami Cookes (9)	62
Amy Smith (10)	63
Lauren Newstead (9)	63
Bethany Stanbridge (10)	63
Sam Brayshaw (9)	64
Amelia Lumb (9)	64
George Hardaker (10)	64
Ella Park (9)	65
Laura Sereena Chawla (10)	65
Carl Place (9)	66
Ryan Olliver (9)	66

Horbury Bridge CE J&I Primary School

Lauren Hammill (9)	67
Kelsey Verity (9)	67
Connor Gosnay (8)	67
Victoria Wilson (7)	67
Ben Terry (7)	68
Lucy Tolson (8)	68
Luke Rogerson (7)	68
Hollie Senior (8)	68
Jack Lonsdale (8)	69
Megan Schofield (7)	69
Millie Fowles (8)	70
Claire Crow (9)	70
Thomas Barber (9)	71
Jason Barber (8)	71
Olivia Allott (7)	71
Nikki Lonsdale (9)	72
Eleanor Mitchell (10)	72
Bradley Gearey (10)	72

Damian Brayshaw (11)	73
Herbie Naylor Mayers (11)	73
Ryan Verity (10)	74
Amy Cudworth (11)	74
Jamie Lamont (11)	74
Natalie Cudworth (9)	75
Matthew Evans (10)	75

Inglebrook School

Ellis Birkby (10)	76
Ashleigh Brain (10)	76
Lucy Fox (10)	77
Thomas Copley (10)	77
James Harrison (9)	78
Rachel Connell (10)	78
Ashley Elliott (10)	78
Lewis Waring (9)	79
Michael Ellis (9)	79
Hadley Stringer (11)	79
Sophie Astle (11)	80
Andrew Earnshaw (10)	80
Amrit Bance (10)	80
Alice Sandham (10)	81
Rachel Cook (10)	81
Laura Pindar (10)	82

Manston St James Primary School

Hannah Shields (11)	82
Rachel MacFadyen (10)	82
Rachael Kennedy (10)	83
Rebecca Hardy (11)	84
Jayshree Chudasama (11)	84

Menston Primary School

Dominic Martill (10)	85
Alice Harrison & Megan Smith (10)	85
Jacob Bentley (10)	85
Hannah Hartley (11)	86
Adam Dinsdale (11)	86
Samuel Akroyd (10)	86

Bethany Sunderland (11)	87
Hannah Montague-Millar & Olivia Winter (10)	87
Alex Bowman (10)	87
Katie Bailey & Ruth Hobley (10)	88
Mercedes Green (11)	88
William Betts (10)	88
Nathan Shields & Jordan Bentley (10)	89
Ellie English (11)	89
Eleanor Midgley & Lana Hutton (10)	90
Emily Cooper & Lisa Emsley (10)	90
Lauren Scaife (11)	90
Yuqing Jiang & David Ratcliffe (10)	91
Ross Hammond (11)	91

Roberttown J&I CE (C) School

Calum Miller (8)	91
Joseph Kerr (8)	92
Bethany Ruston (9)	92
Hannah Mather (10)	93
Thomas Dixon (11)	93
Charlotte Glaves (8)	94
Jessica Mott (11)	95
Chloe Armitage (8)	95
Amy Peacock (9)	95
Josef Balach (11)	96
Ben Tillotson (10)	96
Lexy Clavin (10)	97
Shelby Hutchison & Abigail Binns (10)	97
Melissa Wallis (9)	98
Matthew Stone (10)	98
Mica Jade Gallagher (10)	98
Sam Sessions (11)	99
Andrew Lenk (8)	99
Siobhan Brogden (11)	100
James Enevoldson (11)	100
Beth Armson (9)	101
James Sutcliffe (10)	101
Kerry Brooks (10)	102
Louisa Binns (11)	102
Alex Shaw (10)	103
Sam Purssell (10)	103

Emmeline Robinson (7)	103
Abigail Wallis & Natasha Riches (10)	104
Kerry Murphy (10)	105
Georgia Trevitt	105
Alasdair Hurst (10)	106
Ella Pearson-Glover (8)	107
Megan Cunliffe (10)	107
Will Banyard (7)	107
Christopher Thomas (11)	108
Stevie Chanteleau (8)	108
Hannah Pickering (9)	109
Megan Preston (8)	109
Joel Robinson (7)	109
Liam Gallagher (8)	110
Danielle Cornforth (7)	110
Jack David Collins (10)	111
Jamie Crowther (7)	111
Bethany Robinson (9)	112
Oliver Hedges-Hemingway (8)	112
Helen Edmond (8)	112
Jack Baldwin (9)	113
Jonathan Pickering (7)	113
Megan Enevoldson (8)	113
Sara-Jayne Pollard (10)	114
Jordan Brunt (8)	114
Simon J Gray (10)	115
Eva Hague (7)	115
Laura Baldwin (11)	115
Kirsty Crowther (9)	116
Matthew Brook (10)	116
Billie Terry (8)	116
Amy Blackburn (8)	117
Laylaa Whittaker (9)	117
Sonnie Terry (9)	118
Matthew Haigh (7)	118
Jarda Clayton (7)	119
Katie Miller (11)	119
Lauren Kitson (8)	119
Robyn Michaela Smith (10)	120
Kerry Busby (11)	121
Tom Allatt (11)	122
Rachel Glaves (6)	122

Isabel Oldroyd (7) — 123
George Bartle (7) — 123
Joseph Lancaster (8) — 123

St Ignatius Catholic Primary School, Ossett
Rachel Brook (10) — 124
Catherine Thompson (11) — 124
Siobhan Ann Crossland (11) — 125
Leo Hughes (11) — 125
Caitlin Davies (10) — 126
Nicola Perkins & Joseph Finnigan (11) — 126
Matthew Lowrey (10) — 127

St Mary's CE School, Boston Spa
Phoebe Williams (8) — 127
James Hibbert (10) — 128
Amy Uttley (8) — 128
Cordelia Keston (9) — 129
Alexander Hibbert (7) — 130
Bradley Kitching (8) — 131
Polly Whitelam (9) — 131
Eve McQuillan (10) — 132
James Coates (8) — 133
Jessica Heaton (7) — 133
Natalie Heaton (10) — 134
Naomi Barrow (9) — 134
Roxanne Frost (7) — 135
Emma Whitaker (8) — 135
Jonathan Barrow (8) — 135
Eleri Dorsett-Paynton (7) — 136
Grace Barrett (9) — 136
Jamie Taylor (8) — 136
Liam Livesley (9) — 137
Philip Rodger (11) — 138
Joshua Kidd (8) — 138
Kate Towns (8) — 139
Léonie Ricard (7) — 139
Naomi Allan (11) — 140
Matthew Bulley (9) — 140

Sacred Heart RC Primary School
Bethany Horner (10)	141
Lili Cordingley (9)	141
Amie Scott (10)	142
Samantha Rudge (9)	142
Micheala Mason (10)	143
Jake Brown (9)	143
Joshua Berry (9)	144
Lucy Mitchell (9)	144
Joseph Milner (9)	145
Joe Fletcher (9)	146
Alexander Wilson (9)	146
Darrell Bingham (10)	147
Peter Green (10)	147
Robert Whitaker (10)	148

Sicklinghall CP School
Jemimah Crockford (9)	148
Hetty Yoxall (11)	149
James Woodhams (9)	149
Kali Popely (9)	150
Naomi Probert (9)	151
Lucie Almond (10)	152
Olivia Giddings (9)	153
Jamie Horwell (8)	153
George Barton (9)	154

Stanley St Peter's Primary School
Sophie Beeching-Smith (10)	154
Rebecca Doyle (10)	155
Bethany Riding (10)	156
Bethany Holroyd (11)	157
Robert Newiss (10)	158
Katie Baigent (10)	158
Lauren Fawcett (11)	159
Toni Mees (9)	159
Megan Croxall (11)	160
Helen Dwyer (10)	160
Kirsty Palmer (10)	161
Kieran Wright (10)	161

Georgia Leigh Harris (10)	161
Sam Green (10)	162
Emma Coupland (10)	162
Abigail Couldwell (10)	163
Amy Shipley (10)	163
Hannah Brown (10)	164

The Whartons Primary School

Abigail Hilditch (11)	164
Emma Phimister (11)	165
Katherine Quinn (7)	165
Philip Britteon (10)	166
Jack Richings (10)	167
Jodie Swift (10)	167
Bethan Grubb (9)	168
Sarah Campbell (10)	168
Kelly Thomas (10)	169
Amy Wilson (10)	169
Emma Hartley (7)	169
Rebecca Jane Thomas (8)	170
Olivia Coyle (8)	170
Daniel Atkinson (8)	171
Jordon Lawrence (7)	171

Towngate Primary School

Alex William Holmes (9)	172
Joshua Ward (9)	173
William Ward (9)	173
Chloe Taylor (8)	174
Conner Chappell (8)	174
Joe Batchelor (9)	175
Kimberley Goulthorp (9)	176
Toni Labourn (9)	177
Thomas Kershaw (8)	177
Jordana Standage (9)	178
Kimara Parfitt (8)	178
Thomas English (8)	179
Emma Stoner (9)	179
Charlotte Auty (8)	180
Daniel Stephenson (8)	180
Tom Pitchforth (8)	181

Philippa Bayford (9)	181
Kirsty Scott (8)	182
Toni-Lee Edwards (9)	183
Joshua Leach (8)	183
Aaron Peters (8)	184
Annie Peake (8)	184
Aimee Louise Kershaw (9)	185
Caroline Lewis (8)	185
Harry English (8)	186
Amelia Ann Clayton (9)	186
Richard Athorne (8)	187
Charley Sheard (8)	187
Blythe Senior (8)	188

The Poems

My Magic Box
(Based on 'Magic Box' by Kit Wright)

I will put in my box . . .
A kitten's fur,
The colourful sunset at night-time,
A soft, silky, furry puppy.

I will put in my box . . .
Fireworks flickering from past festivals,
A baby's first step,
The taste of a fresh, juicy apple.

I will put in my box . . .
A silky, soft snowflake,
A dragon that blows out ice.

Alexandra Horner (9)
Ash Grove J&I School

The Lifeguard
(In the style of 'The Highwayman' by Alfred Noyes)

The scorching hot sun was firing down at the beach,
The sun was setting upon the dark blue seas,
The beach was as gold as ever,
And the lifeguard came running - running - running,
The lifeguard came running up to the dark blue sea.

She wore a pink top, with a silver necklace at her chin,
With a jingle and her jewellery twinkled
And she rode with a twinkle, her necklace hardly twinkled,
Her nicely coloured trainers sparkled in the brightly coloured sun.

Bethany Hammond (9)
Ash Grove J&I School

The Beast Trainer
(In the style of 'The Highwayman' by Alfred Noyes)

The mist was a hazy breath
Among the feet of the trees.
The moon was quietly hiding behind a cloudy breeze,
The forest was a never-ending green maze
And the beast trainer came tiptoeing, tiptoeing, tiptoeing,
The beast trainer came tiptoeing under the moon's gaze.

She had leather trousers, tightly made for her legs
And a thick green vest made of suede,
Of which would never rip.
She tiptoed very silent,
She whispered very silent
As she got ready to use her whip!

Over the puddles she searched and wandered
In the forest ever so dark,
What was that noise?
The cry of a lark?
What was that sound? She turned around,
Flashing her long black locks,
A whimper!
A whimper!
From his den there jumped out the cub of a fox!

Tyler Duke (9)
Ash Grove J&I School

The Dog Walker
(In the style of 'The Highwayman' by Alfred Noyes)

The sun was blazing down through the cotton wool clouds.
The time of day the ice cream men come so there are lots of crowds.
The street was a lane of glamour shining in the sun.
The dog walker came walking - walking - walking.
The dog walker came after a day of fun.
He wore a pink fluffy jumper and a purple scruffy scarf,
Trousers that went over his heels and trainers made out of calf.

Danielle Thomas (9)
Ash Grove J&I School

My Magic Box
(Based on 'Magic Box' by Kit Wright)

I will put in my box . . .
The first tweet of a baby bird
The fairy lights' twinkle on the Christmas tree
Soft fur of a purring kitten

I will put in my box . . .
My first birthday wish coming to me
The first look out of my eyes
Friends that help me with my work

I will put in my box . . .
Fresh water from a nearby well
A verse of a song
A rule from my mum

My box is fashioned from diamonds and rubies
It has moons on the roof
With stars in the corners
Its hinges are the coldness of ice.

Jessica Tetlow (9)
Ash Grove J&I School

My Magic Box
(Based on 'Magic Box' by Kit Wright)

I will put in the box . . .
The sea swaying on a soft snowy winter's morning,
The tip of a toe touching the water,
The wind blowing through my hair.

I will put in the box . . .
The first sound of my sister,
My grandma Jill,
Cookies that have just been made.

Frazer Hawkins (9)
Ash Grove J&I School

My Magic Box
(Based on 'Magic Box' by Kit Wright)

I shall put in my box . . .
A begging dog desperate for dinner
A F1 car sliding into the side of a racetrack
And the soft sound of a kitten.

I shall put in my box . . .
The sound of an aeroplane that's just taking off
The taste of a fresh picked apple
And the sight of an African elephant.

My box is fashioned with
Sharks' teeth for the handle
Snakes for the hinges
And some wishes in the corners.

Kane Appleton (9)
Ash Grove J&I School

The Magic Box
(Based on 'Magic Box' by Kit Wright)

I will put in my box . . .
A drill screeching through metal
The spray of a windsurfer
The feel of a wet boom on a windsurfer

I will put in my box . . .
The feel of the steering wheel on a forklift
The sound of trees rustling in the midnight wind
The feel of wood vibrating as it splits between the saw

My box is designed from tarmac and coal, gold and TFR
I will windsurf in my box on the rough Hawaiian sea.

Jared Armstrong (9)
Ash Grove J&I School

My Magic Box
(Based on 'Magic Box' by Kit Wright)

I will put in my box . . .
The swish of swaying trees on a summer's day,
A snap of the jaws of a vicious crocodile,
The touch of a silky, slithery snake.

I will put in my box . . .
The crunch of snow on Christmas morning,
The views of the beautiful countryside,
The first step of a baby.

I will put in my box . . .
The sound of waves crashing on the rocks,
The last word of my grandmother,
A conker out of its shell.

My box is woven from rubies, diamonds and emeralds
With a chunk of planet Mercury in each corner
And the heat of the sun on the lid,
The hinges are the finger joints of a dinosaur.

Lewis Germain (9)
Ash Grove J&I School

Jet Skier
(In the style of 'The Highwayman' by Alfred Noyes)

The sun was a fading ball in the evening light
The lake was smooth and glittering in the dusky night
The rocks rose from the sea's floor
And the jet skier was revving, revving, revving
The jet skier was revving to the rocky shore.

Christopher Pagdin (9)
Ash Grove J&I School

My Magic Box
(Based on 'Magic Box' by Kit Wright)

I will put in my box . . .
A cat miaowing as it chases a mouse,
A snowman sparkling silver with snowflakes,
The soft, silky fur of a small puppy.

I will put in my box . . .
The loud roar of a lion,
The waves of the sea crashing onto the land,
The whizzing sounds of fireworks.

I will put in my box . . .
The taste of a juicy orange,
The glowing ray of the sun,
The sharp teeth of a shark.

Danny Vaquero (9)
Ash Grove J&I School

I Love Animals
(Onomatopoeic poem)

The grunt of the pig,
The roar of the lions,
The screech of the elephant,
The slurp of the giraffe,
The growl of the tiger,
The neigh of the horse,
The howl of the dog,
The miaow of the cat,
The pecking of the woodpecker,
The squeak of the rabbit.

Bethany Hirst (10)
Ash Grove J&I School

Magic Box
(Based on 'Magic Box' by Kit Wright)

I will put in the box . . .
The purr of a pouncing kitten on a passing night,
A little puppy asleep on someone's knee,
A touch of a smooth silky snake.

I will put in the box . . .
The smell of fresh bread, crispy and brown,
The last bark of an ancient dog,
The love of my mum and dad.

I will put in the box . . .
The shiniest star,
The call of an owl,
A birthday.

My box will be built up with
Snakes, thunder and demons,
With worms for hinges
And wishes in the corners.

I shall take my box everywhere
In the biggest shop of the busiest town.

Jon Downing (9)
Ash Grove J&I School

I Love Weather
(Onomatopoeic poem)

The crack of the thunder
The flash of the lightning
The sizzle of the sun
The patter of rain
The plod of snow
The twinkle of the fog
The fluff of the clouds.

Bradley Bateman (10)
Ash Grove J&I School

The Magic Box
(Based on 'Magic Box' by Kit Wright)

I will put in the box . . .
The cool calming Caribbean sea,
The colours of a rainbow on a hot rainy day,
The touch of a hand on a harmless dog.

I will put in the box . . .
A sheep leaping over high hills,
A wish from a small boy,
The sound of a horse.

I will put in the box . . .
The bright romantic colours of fireworks,
The quietness of a deserted street,
A welcoming smile from my mum.

My box is fashioned from the feathered peacock,
Snow from the ground,
White fluffy clouds
And the hinges are the teeth of a lion.

Danielle Foulds (9)
Ash Grove J&I School

I Love Animals
(Onomatopoeic poem)

The roar of the lions.
The cheep of the chicks.
The hiss of the snakes.
The twitter of the birds.
The wail of the elephants.
The squeak of the bats.
The growl of the bears.
The squawk of the parrots.
The snap of the alligator.
The purr of the cats.

Danielle Haigh (10)
Ash Grove J&I School

Eskimo
(In the style of 'The Highwayman' by Alfred Noyes)

Icy cold snow tumbled onto drifts already on the ground,
Red-hot sun was a big fireball twisting around,
The ice was as smooth as glass.
The Eskimo came sliding - sliding - sliding,
The Eskimo came sliding to the cold igloo door.

Soft, cuddly mittens, nice, warm, woolly trousers,
She'd a thick, soft, fur coat on.
Her skis were very shiny,
Her poles were very glittery - glittery - glittery.
Her poles were very glittery under a winter sun.

Megan Hemingway (10)
Ash Grove J&I School

The Magic Box
(Based on 'Magic Box' by Kit Wright)

I will put in my box . . .
Fire sizzling on a cold night
A snowman melting in the sun
A dog's paw on your hand.

I will put in my box . . .
My brother when he laughs
The thought of snow on my hand
The first cry of a baby being born.

My box will be made out of metal and steel.

Bradley Dwyer (9)
Ash Grove J&I School

I Love . . . Fruit
(Onomatopoeic poem)

The drip of orange juice going into my mouth.
The drop of lemon making my mouth sour.
The crunch of apples tickling my taste buds.
The munch of tomatoes when they enter my mouth.
The slurp of blackcurrant when I drink out of my cup.
The squashiness of bananas when they are chopped up.
The crunch of a pear, fully ripe.

Daniel Ingham (10)
Ash Grove J&I School

I Love Fishing
(Onomatopoeic poem)

The splash of the fish
The tug of the rod
The sadness of the fish getting away
The tweeting of the birds
The silence of the lake
The screech of the reel
The plop of fish.

Andrew Mapston (10)
Ash Grove J&I School

Falling Asleep

Motorbikes buzzing when the day passes on
Wind chimes whistling in the breeze of the night
Trees rustling, restless in the darkness
The house is still and quiet
Footsteps on the path
The chinking of bottles and glass
Beep, beep, beep goes the alarm.

Curtis Cowell (9)
Ash Grove J&I School

The Water Baby
(In the style of 'The Highwayman' by Alfred Noyes)

The sun like a sparkling teardrop shining through the sea.
The sea as free as free can be.
The seaweed is rows of wavy hair amongst the sandy bay
And the water baby came floating - floating - floating
Up to her cosy bed he lay.
She'd a pearl braided necklace and a diamond belly button ring.
Long golden hair and a voice set to sing!
She floated with a gold twinkle on her skin not even a wrinkle
Her pearl necklace a twinkle under the peaceful sea!
Over the coral reef she went on, a giant white pearl she lent.
She sung a very merry tune and who should be waiting there?
But all the fish of the coral reef!
All the fish in the coral reef!
Who had now pulled up a chair.

Sam Whitehouse (9)
Ash Grove J&I School

I Love Nature
(Onomatopoeic poem)

The rustle of the bushes.
The croak of the frogs.
The hums of the hummingbirds.
The pitter-patter of the raindrops.
The whooshes of the wind.
The squawk of the parrots.
The howl of the wolf.
The *sshh* of the river.
The growl of the bear.
The boing of the bunnies.

Hannah Stoppard (10)
Ash Grove J&I School

The Magic Box
(Based on 'Magic Box' by Kit Wright)

I will put in the box . . .
The soft, sweet purr of a kitten.
Squirrels jumping from tree to tree.
The soft, silky fur of a rabbit.

I will put in the box . . .
The laughter of my parents.
The splash of the waves gently flowing onto a beach.
The multicoloured flames on a fire.

I will put in the box . . .
A baby's first smile.
The Australian Outback.
A baby koala bear.

Melissa Cocliff (9)
Ash Grove J&I School

I Love Animals
(Onomatopoeic poems)

The bark of puppies.
The miaow of kittens.
The neigh of horses.
The roar of lions.
The squeak of squirrels.
The splash of dolphins.
The snap of the sharks.
The bubble of fish.
The roar of bears.
The crunch of giraffes eating.

I love animals.

Shannen Hall (10)
Ash Grove J&I School

My Magic Box
(Based on 'Magic Box' by Kit Wright)

I will put in the box . . .
The sound of a loud trumpet
A big colourful rainbow on a rainy day
The soft touch of my bed.

I will put in the box . . .
A dog whining for his dinner
Somebody's wish
A cup full of squash.

I will put in the box . . .
A colourful firework shooting up in the air
The sound of a grunting pig

My box is fashioned from fire and silver
The hinges are of sharks' teeth
And secrets in the corner.

Ben Broad (9)
Ash Grove J&I School

I Love Night-Time
(Onomatopoeic poem)

I love night-time.
The tweet of an owl.
The howl of a wolf far away in the distance.
The whistle of the wind.
The rustle of the trees.
The snore of my dad.
The *waah* of the baby next door.
The ringing of my alarm clock.
I love night-time.

Caitlin Smaldon (10)
Ash Grove J&I School

The Policeman
(In the style of 'The Highwayman' by Alfred Noyes)

The wind drifts all around the dark sky.
The moon is like a light bulb shining in the dark sky.
The path was a river running down the street
And the policeman came plodding, plodding, plodding.
His pulse was a tremendous beat.
He wore a black hat with a gold badge on it
And black pointy shoes.
A black top and gold buttons.

Jake Bench (10)
Ash Grove J&I School

I Love . . . The Sea
(Onomatopoeic poem)

The splash of a dolphin.
The clash of waves.
The bubble of sea creatures swimming away.
The munch of fishes eating seaweed.
The bubble of a fish.
The munch of a shark eating a squid.
The patter of rain on the water.

Roxanne Adamson (10)
Ash Grove J&I School

I Love Football
(Onomatopoeic poem)

The roar of the crowd.
The thud of the ball.
The squelch of the pitch.
The splash of the water bottle.
The rustle of the grass.
The crunch of the player.
The whistle of the ref.

Lewis Philips (10)
Ash Grove J&I School

The Barmaid
(In the style of 'The Highwayman' by Alfred Noyes)

The thunder was like a drum that was stuck in the sky.
The moon was the only light in mid-July.
The pebbled path was a string of moonlight under the moonlit sky
And the barmaid came walking - walking - walking
And the barmaid came walking up to the old bar door.

She'd a long white apron around her waist
And she carried an old rusty key with no haste.
It fitted with never a scratch: her heels came to the knee
And she walked without a sound.
Her rusty key made no sound.
Her apron flew, no sound under the little rusty key.

Heather Andrew (9)
Ash Grove J&I School

I Love The Sound Of The Animals
(Onomatopoeic poem)

I love the chirp of the bird.
I love the bark of the dog.
I love the miaow of the cat.
I love the moo of the cow.
I love the grunt of the pig.
I love the baa of the sheep.
I love the bubble of the fish.
I love the howl of the wolf.

Lewis Clark (10)
Ash Grove J&I School

I Love Animals
(Onomatopoeic poem)

The twitter of the birds.
The laughing of the hyena.
The trumpet of the elephant.
The roar of the lion.
The neigh of the mustangs.
The moo of the cow.
The miaow of the cat.
The squeak of the squirrel.
The snapping of the crocodile.
The growl of the bear.

Ashley Daykin (10)
Ash Grove J&I School

I Love . . . McDonald's
(Onomatopoeic poem)

The sizzle of chips being fried.
The lick of a Smarties McFlurry.
The slurp of a Coke.
The munch of a Big Mac meal.
The crunch of a chicken nugget.
The plop of ice cream.
The whistle of the serving assistants.

Michael Kirby (10)
Ash Grove J&I School

I Love Food
(Onomatopoeic poem)

The munch of apples.
The sizzle of bacon.
The rustle of crisps.
The crunch of toast.
The bubble of pasta.
The crackle of cornflakes.
The slurp of soup.
The squelch of jelly.
The crunch of lettuce.
The fizz of pop.

Hayley Lockett (10)
Ash Grove J&I School

I Love Cricket
(Onomatopoeic poem)

The boom of the bat
The smash of the wickets
The thud of the catch
The whizz of the ball
The hit of the pads
The roar of the crowd
Howzat!

Liam Rollin (10)
Ash Grove J&I School

I Love Food
(Onomatopoeic poem)

The pop of a pea
The crunch of a crisp
The splat of the yoghurt
The slurp of the soup
The crack of the coconut
The munch of an apple
The sizzle of the bacon
The fizz of the pop
The crackle of the Rice Krispies
The pop-pop of the popcorn.

Jake Thomas (10)
Ash Grove J&I School

I Love My Niece
(Onomatopoeic poem)

I love my niece
The waaing of my niece
The moaning of my niece
The squeak of my niece's dummy
The glug of my niece's bottle
The rattle of my niece's toy
The *aachoo* of my niece's sneezes
The splutter of my niece's coughing.

Amy Evans (10)
Ash Grove J&I School

I Love Food
(Onomatopoeic poem)

The sizzle of sausages
The bubble of potatoes
The pop of popcorn
The crunch of toast
The munch of Mars bars
The slurp of cream
The crack of eggs
I love food.

Samuel Womersley (10)
Ash Grove J&I School

It's Not The Same Anymore

It's not the same since Nana Boyes went up
Families are families
Never been, never gone.

It's not the same anymore
Her belongings are still,
The urge to see them is no more.

It's not the same anymore
I can't bring myself to think about her,
There's no reason now.

Her cups hang on trees,
Her other belongings in drawers and cupboards.

It's not the same now I can't see her,
I can't hear her anymore.

My memories of her make me sad,
Though she's gone she's still with me.
When I watch Songs of Praise I cry and cry.

It's not the same without my Nana Boyes.

Emily Benton (9)
Bramley St Peter's CE Primary School

My Magic Box
(Based on 'Magic Box' by Kit Wright)

I will put in my box . . .

The memory of a photograph of
My mum and dad getting engaged.

My auntie Angie getting married,
When my grandma Chewy died.

I will put in my box . . .

A photograph of my nan's lost laugh
Five years ago and a memory of my grandad,
A piece of jet-black fur from my dog.

I will put in my box . . .

A lovely piece of my work,
A drop of sweat from my grandma Chewy,
A piece of sand from Scarborough.

I will put in my box . . .

A picture that my grandad drew me,
A bobble that my grandma bought me,
A video that my mum gave me.

My box is made of out of gold, silver
And iron and stainless steel.

My box will take me to Bridlington against
The sandy beach and the bright blue sky.

Kimberley Carrick (9)
Bramley St Peter's CE Primary School

I Like . . .

I like fish also chips,
I like grapes without the pips.

I like Mummy, she's so nice,
I like curry without the rice.

I like bread and tomato soup,
I like the playground without the hoop.

I like cats they're so purry,
I like rabbits they're so furry.

I like cute little dogs,
I like mucky, round logs.

I like lovely, licky lollies,
I like the girls named Polly.

I like a big, bubbly bath,
I like to have a big laugh.

I like to cook my tea in a pan,
I like a big fake tan.

Katie Fahy (10)
Bramley St Peter's CE Primary School

Crocodile

A crocodile has very rough skin.
It has sharp teeth
Dark rough skin.
Crocodiles have needle-sharp fingernails.
They have very long tails.
They are heavy and have got dark skin.

Camille Reed (10)
Bramley St Peter's CE Primary School

The Dragon

The dragon is a creature that flies about at night
If you're out at your friend's house he'll give you a nasty fright
With green scaly skin
Teeth as sharp as a pin
Fire for breath
He's sure to bring death
The princess' screams
Like the dragons, are only in dreams.

Reece Harrison (9)
Bramley St Peter's CE Primary School

Dragons

D ragons are nasty
R ude dragons hate people
A ll dragons breathe fire
G iant dragons are fierce
O range flames blow out
N o dragons like people.

Dale Reece Oyston (9)
Bramley St Peter's CE Primary School

The Animals

H edgehogs are spiky it is probably the most spiky animal I know.
O striches are so brave that they can put their heads in the sand.
R abbits can see in the dark and they have bushy tails.
S nakes shed their skin and smell with their tongues.
E lephants are so fat they can squash you.

Ariane Daniels (9)
Bramley St Peter's CE Primary School

The Magic Box
(Based on 'Magic Box' by Kit Wright)

I will put into the box . . .
A memory of my uncle's wedding,
A memory of my hamster
And the memory of my friends at my old school.

I will put into the box . . .
A memory of my first tooth,
A memory of my first holiday in Greece
And my first Christmas.

I will put into the box . . .
A memory of my first photo,
A memory of the smiles on my best holiday
And the laughter of my second birthday,
A memory of my first kiss from my parents.

I will put into the box . . .
A memory of my first tear,
A memory of the fright from my scary dream
And my scary accident when I got taken down to the hospital,
A memory of my first teddy bear.

My box is fashioned from tigers' fur
With a twinkling star
And the scented rose petals and red rubies
From the darkest coal mine in the world.

I shall go dancing in my box on a sparkling stage
With a disco ball shining like the sun.

Gemma Louise Kennally (9)
Bramley St Peter's CE Primary School

May I Be

May I be the person who people follow
May I be solid not hollow.

May I be the butterfly who never dies
May I be a fairy who forever flies.

May I be the person who never gets old
May I be a paper that will never fold.

May I be calm not hot
May I be a stained glass window not a teapot.

May I be always right
May I be spreading peace, even at night.

May I be a blooming flower
May I be a plant having a yellow-drop shower.

May I be a unicorn with a gold horn
May I be a bronze statue of a fawn.

May I be a secret that's never been spoken
May I be a circuit that's never been broken.

May I be forever spreading peace
May I be everything that everyone seeks.

Tanieka Kargwal (10)
Bramley St Peter's CE Primary School

Hummingbird Haiku

Hummingbird hovers,
Above the bright pink flower,
He takes a long sip.

Eleanor Davies (9)
Bramley St Peter's CE Primary School

The Magic Box
(Based on 'Magic Box' by Kit Wright)

I will put into the box . . .
The smile of my nana,
The kindness of my mum,
The fur of my dead rabbit Mike,
The fur of my two cats.

I will put into the box . . .
The remembrance of my great grandma,
The remembrance of my rabbit Caspar,
A horse show,
A photograph of my grandad.

I will put into the box . . .
The antlers of a reindeer,
A lock of my sister's hair,
A drop of Brid's sea.

My box is made of the king's jewels,
Some shells off the beach,
Moonstones on the lid,
Unicorn horns as the hinges
And a hard padlock to seal it.

Jake Nevison (10)
Bramley St Peter's CE Primary School

Congratulations

A daughter's joy can warm your heart,
She's got you from the very start,
With dress up clothes and hair to curl,
Congratulations it's a girl.

Hannah Fawcett (9)
Bramley St Peter's CE Primary School

My Magic Box
(Based on 'Magic box' by Kit Wright)

I will put in my box . . .

A smile of my grandma and grandad,
The last laugh of my uncle Eddy,
The cry of my cat Blue.

I will put into my box . . .

A horse's shiny hoof,
The picture of my little sister before she went
And a golden cross that my grandma had.

I will put into my box . . .

A pair of my old trainers,
A glowing space rock that sparkles,
The beak of a wishing robin
And the cry of a whale.

My box is made out of gold that cannot break,
Shiny silver straps and iron as strong as anything.

Ted Thompson-Melling (9)
Bramley St Peter's CE Primary School

Football

When you're running down the pitch with great speed.
And the wind is flying through your hair,
Your mum and dad are cheering you on,
And bang . . . ! Silence, you're watching the ball glide,
Through the air, past the defenders, past the goalkeeper, then,
Goal!

Joseph Pearson (10)
Bramley St Peter's CE Primary School

It's Not The Same Anymore

It's not the same anymore
Since Grahame has gone
I miss the way he used to tickle me.

It's not the same anymore
I miss the way he used to give me a piggyback
I just don't feel the same anymore.

It's not the same anymore
He went without saying goodbye
I don't feel comfortable anymore
It does not feel the same without him.

It's not the same anymore
Since Grahame has gone
I miss the way he used to tickle me.

Christina Storey (9)
Bramley St Peter's CE Primary School

The Magic Box
(Based on 'Magic Box' by Kit Wright)

I will put into the box . . .
The crown of the King and Queen,
The horn of a rhino,
The wing of a butterfly.

I will put into the box . . .
The claws of a tiger,
The leg of the Iron Man,
A bone of a dinosaur,
The stars of the night.

Aaran Whitehead (10)
Bramley St Peter's CE Primary School

It's Not The Same Anymore: A Eulogy To An Animal

It's not the same since Snoopy died.
Carrots are carrots.
Never ran, never fetched.

It's not the same anymore.
Vegetables lying still and lifeless.
The urge to eat them is gone.

It's not the same now.
I can't bring myself to eat vegetables.
There's no reason to do so.

His name stands on a cross
And his colour is in my mind.

His hat and bowl just standing there
Lying at the back of the garage.

My fingers will never be chewed
And I have no use for playing now.

I can now watch TV without him
Scratching the hut.

I don't have to clean him out anymore
And never feel the wet water on him.

It's just not the same anymore.
When Snoopy died, a small part of me died.

All that's left is bones and rust
And his cross standing in the garden.

Matthew Stitch (10)
Bramley St Peter's CE Primary School

Tigers

T igers are very wise when they hunt their prey.
I n the swaying green grass.
G rowling at the moon.
E ating day and night.
R unning step by step.

Bryoni Alderson (10)
Bramley St Peter's CE Primary School

I Like Cricket

I like cricket
I like cricket
I like playing with my mates

I like batting
I like batting
I like batting the ball

I like bowling
I like bowling
I like bowling at the wickets

I hate losing
I hate losing
I hate losing to my mates

I love winning
I love winning
I love winning against my mates

I like cricket
I like cricket
I like playing with my mates.

Jamie Baxter (11)
Brotherton and Byram CP School

My Big Sister

On Monday she's on the phone
On Tuesday she's all alone
On Wednesday she does nothing but moan
On Thursday she took the dog's bone
On Friday she eats an ice cream cone
On Saturday she stays at home
But on Sunday she's not on the phone
She's not alone
She's not having a moan
Or taking the dog's bone
Or eating an ice cream cone
And she's not alone at home
She's not here, she's not there, she's not anywhere!

Gemma Brooks (10)
Brotherton and Byram CP School

Shopping

I like shopping for myself
Trying on clothes
Finding some shoes then you can't lose.

I like shopping for make-up
Pick up some blusher
To make me look lusher
Me and my blush.

I don't like shopping for food
Walking round and round the aisles
It always puts me in a bad mood.

Charlotte Heale (10)
Brotherton and Byram CP School

Pets

Chloe's got a dog
Who always chases frogs.
Zoe's got a cat
Her brother's got a rat.

Leane's got a snake
Who lives in a lake.
Charlie's got a fox
Who was found in a box.

Josh has got a goldfish
Which is called Trish.
Sarah's got a guinea pig
Who once wore a wig.

Hannah Price (10)
Brotherton and Byram CP School

My Holiday

Last year, I went on holiday
It was OK, even though I had to pay!

We bought an ice cream from a stall
'Yum-yum,' bragged my brother Paul.

Then we walked onto the beach
My dad's face was like a peach!

'Come on, slow coach,' yelled my dad
I was walking behind looking sad.

Now I can look back to the past
And my memories always last!

Natalie Clough (10)
Brotherton and Byram CP School

Shopping's Brill!

Shopping's brill
You need lots of skill,
So grab your phone
And find a good tone,
Put all the clothes in the trolley,
But don't forget the brolly.

Lots of stuff to wear
And don't forget to stay fair,
People love to shop,
Wearing a gorgeous top,
Use all your money
And remember to stay funny!

Buy some gorgeous tops
Go in all the expensive shops!

Laura Golding (11)
Brotherton and Byram CP School

Shopping

I love shopping
With all my mates
We all started hopping
But we always are too late!

I love shopping
Going round and round
We all started popping
On the dusty ground!

I love shopping
Not with my mam
She always starts mopping
And she loves to eat ham!

Autumn Newby (10)
Brotherton and Byram CP School

Fireworks Poem

F antastic
I ncredible
R ockets
E rupts
W icked
O rbital
R ockets
K aboom
S izzling.

Tanya Williamson (10)
Brotherton and Byram CP School

Girls

We are girls
We get to wear pearls
We buy them at the shops
Along with lollipops.

We girls are great
We hang out with our mates
In the sunlight it is quite bright
We have a sleepover at night.

Aquilla Berenice Softley (10)
Brotherton and Byram CP School

Count To Five

One chicken is watching TV
Two ponies are playing CDs
Three pigs grooving on the dance mat
Who's on the karaoke? (Oh no it's the cat!)
Four rabbits on the PlayStation
Five dogs on their snowboards having lots of fun.

Lauren Clisby (10)
Brotherton and Byram CP School

Shopping

I love shopping
It is great
Best if you go
With your mate.

Lots and lots
And lots of shops,
Buy new skirts
Buy new tops.

Me and my friends
Love to shop.
Love to shop
Until we drop.

The White Rose
Is my favourite place.
It is cool
It is great.

I like spending
Lots of money
When it's raining,
When it's sunny.

I go shopping
In ice or snow.
When it's windy
And when it blows.

Lauren Ramsey (10)
Brotherton and Byram CP School

But 11

When I was one
I ate a bun
When I was two
I didn't have a clue
When I was three
I swallowed a bee
When I was four
I went on a grand tour
When I was five
I felt alive
When I was six
I learnt how the clock ticks
When I was seven
I acted eleven
When I was eight
I built a gate
When I was nine
I felt just fine
When I was 10
I made a den
But when I was 11
I was just plain 11.

Devon Croft (11)
Brotherton and Byram CP School

Shopping

I love to shop
I can shop till I drop
I buy shoes and shirts
Trousers and skirts.

New Look and Tammy are the best
But earning the cash is like a huge test
When I go shopping I wear cool tops
And I only go in the expensive shops

So take your bag
But don't forget to look at the tag
Be cool not funny
And use up all your money

I love to shop
I can shop till I drop!

Jodie Tate (11)
Brotherton and Byram CP School

Motorbikes

Flag straight
    Off you go
        Jump high
    Jump low
        Somersault
            Off we go
        Fast as you
        Can
Go
    Through the
        Finish
            Line.

Bradley Hunter (10)
Brotherton and Byram CP School

The Animals' Point Of View!

I don't know, I do care,
Why do humans stand and stare?
All day long they look at me,
I wish, I wish that I was free!

Just for once I wish,
That I was feeding humans fish,
I wish they were peering through the bars
And animals were driving very posh cars!

I know, I know it's only a wish
And that keepers feed the penguins fish
And they named the parrot Sam
And they made the beavers' dam!

I hate the humans, they caught me,
While I was swinging in a tree,
They feed me though it's not that bad,
Still I wish I was with my *dad!*

Nicole Halliday (11)
Brotherton and Byram CP School

Spider

Spider run
Spider small
Spider big
Spider furry
Spider walking
Spider jumping
Spider ugly
Spider wiggling
Spider stinging
Spider eating
Spider biting
Spider crawling
Spider staring at me!
Spider spying.

Thomas Farmer (8)
Carlton Road J&I School

January To December

January brings lots of cheer
As we look forward to a brand new year.

February brings out the showers
No chance of seeing any flowers.

March brings on the spring
And bees come out with their powerful stings.

April is a time for spring
When Mr Bunny comes to bring.

May brings out the flowers
Say goodbye to the April showers.

June brings out the doves
Time to take off our gloves.

July brings out a lamb
Now we get to pick and eat some ham.

August brings out the sun
Let's have a tasty bun.

September brings on the summer
Let's make the place funner.

October brings out autumn
Looking forward to a happy half term.

November brings on a breeze
Time to wrap up so you don't freeze.

December brings on the snow
Now let's go and have a throw.

Joshua Mitchell (9)
Carlton Road J&I School

Lion

Lion running
Lion roaring
Lion hides
Lion catching
Lion eating
Lion clawing
Lion scary
Lion creeps.

Morgan Williams (8)
Carlton Road J&I School

My Teacher

My teacher's pretty,
My teacher's singing,
My teacher's dancing,
My teacher's happy,
My teacher's skipping,
My teacher's joyful,
My lovely teacher!

Kayleigh Varey (9)
Carlton Road J&I School

The Old Beard

In my dad's beard you'll find old minging slobber from his food,
You'll find dry old bogies stuck like glue
And fingernails from last Christmas in 2001.
In my dad's beard you'll find mouldy green meat which is raw,
You'll find maggots from when he was asleep,
In my dad's beard.

Gary Curtis (10)
Carlton Road J&I School

Dad's Beard

In my dad's beard you'll find
Mouldy cheese that has a dark taste
And green colour

You'll find bits of toenails
That he has chewed for an hour
And green and red slimy, slithering bogies
That have gone mouldy.

In my dad's beard you'll find
Pickings of boiled spots
You'll find peeled scabs that
Have been there for five years
And bits of last week's Bolognese
In my dad's beard!

Imogen Copley (10)
Carlton Road J&I School

Spider

Spider web
Spider jump
Spider run
Spider scare
Spider crawl
Spider bite
Spider ugly
Spider look
Spider kill
Spider angry
Spider happy
Spider sad.

Macauly Kolka (9)
Carlton Road J&I School

Dad's Beard

In my dad's beard you'll find . . .
False teeth - the ones he thought he lost last Christmas.
You'll find slimy, sloppy sausages
And pickings of pork pies.

In my dad's beard you'll find . . .
Mouldy chocolate that was there last year!
You'll find 99 spots that he picked when he was 30
And curly clumps of hair
In my dad's beard!

Kelly Sheppard (10)
Carlton Road J&I School

My Puppy

My puppy chewing
My puppy messing
My puppy barking
My puppy annoying
My puppy cleaning
My puppy sleeping
My puppy growling
My puppy.

Rachel Burridge (9)
Carlton Road J&I School

My Brother

My brother silly
My brother clumsy
My brother happy
My brother dancing
My brother funny
My brother ugly
My brother mucky
My brother!

Ryan Lees (9)
Carlton Road J&I School

January To December

January brings us lots of cheer
As we look forward to a brand new year.
February brings the snow
Makes our feet and fingers glow.
March brings us lots of fun
I think it's time to have a big bun.
April is a time for spring
What special present will Mr Bunny bring?
May is a time for a break
I can hardly wait.
June is a time for sun
Makes us all have plenty of fun.
July picks us a new year in school
So we can go in the pool.
August is a time for a holiday
And all our mums can pray.
September is a time for a feast
Made with good stuff and yeast.
October is a time for spells
But watch out some of those smell.
November is a time for fire
Watch the fireworks go higher and higher.
December is a time for celebrating
Makes all the red robins sing, sing, sing.

Lee Sykes (9)
Carlton Road J&I School

Months Of The Year

January brings lots of cheer
As we look forward to a brand new year
February starts to rain
You can't go out, it's a shame
March is time for flowers
Growing outside for hours
April is the time to play
Getting ready for May
May is the month before summer
If you play outside you get rougher
June brings lots of heat
It's too hot to wear anything on your feet
July brings lots of light
Stops people from having a fight
August is the time for a holiday
Wherever you are going it might remind you of May
September leaves are changing colour
The ground is getting fuller and fuller
October is time for Hallowe'en
You can make some music with a tambourine
November brings all the fire
Children can't go round the wire
December is time for Christmas
If you go out you lose your fitness.

Joshua Green (9)
Carlton Road J&I School

January To December

January brings lots of cheer
As we look forward to a brand new year

February makes us snow
Makes our toes and fingers glow

March brings out the sun
So people can have loads of fun

April brings the spring
Makes our birds come out and sing

May brings all the lovely flowers
Leaving behind the April showers

June brings out the sun
So people's faces glow with fun

July brings late light nights
So people can have water fights

August brings all the beers
So people can say cheers!

September makes leaves fall
While people run and kick the ball

October brings all the rain
So people run and fall in pain

November brings Bonfire Night
All the fireworks are so bright

December brings Christmas cheer
Now we can start a new year.

Dionne Dockerty Shields (10)
Carlton Road J&I School

January To December

January brings lots of cheer,
As we look forward to a brand new year.

February brings lots of screams,
When it is Friday thirteenth.

March brings a bit of sun,
When spring has nearly begun.

April brings Easter time,
With roast chicken and a glass of wine.

May brings lovely things,
When the sun's out and the birds sing.

June brings paddling pools,
While my dad's messing with his tools.

July brings lots of shops,
It's hot so we use ice pops.

August is the holiday month,
While we're on the plane eating chocolates and flumps.

September brings brown leaves,
Which are slowly falling off trees.

October brings Hallowe'en,
We give them a sweet when they say trick or treat.

November brings Bonfire Night,
While fireworks light up the sky.

December brings lovely presents
And my mum cooks the pheasant.

Jasmine Evans (9)
Carlton Road J&I School

January To December

January brings lots of cheer,
As we look forward to a brand new year.

February brings the rain and the snow,
Makes our feet and fingers glow.

March brings a bit of sun,
As we go out to have a lot of fun.

April brings Easter time,
We all like a glass of wine.

May brings colourful flowers,
Leaves behind the April showers.

June brings paddling pools,
While my dad mends his car with his box of tools.

July brings lots of mops,
We all like to look in fashion shops.

August brings ice lollies,
My baby sister plays with her dollies.

September brings different coloured leaves,
As they all come tumbling off the trees.

October brings scary masks,
People dare them to do tasks.

November brings Bonfire Night
They let off fireworks, there was a great flash of light.

December brings lots of presents,
We all like to eat a nice roast pheasant.

Jenna Leigh Butterfield (9)
Carlton Road J&I School

Months Of The Year

January brings lots of cheer
As we look forward to a brand new year.

February brings lots of snow
We are trapped in, there is nowhere to go.

March brings loads of rain
As I see it dribbling down a drain.

April. Here comes spring and here comes
A little white bunny and starts to sing.

May. Here comes Mr Sun
As we go out and play it's lots of fun.

June brings lots of joy
When the children play with their toys.

July brings the golden sun
Get our paddling pool out, it's really quite fun.

August is here, we go to the beach
And play in the sun.

September brings the sweaty sun,
We get all sticky it's not really fun.

October here, the children say trick or treat
They give us sweets, it's good to eat.

November brings the light it's really bright
And really fun, the brightness looks like sun.

December brings lots of fun
Presents under the Christmas tree beside the wall.

Lauren Clements (9)
Carlton Road J&I School

January To December

January brings lots of cheers,
That's when my dad mostly goes for a couple of beers.

February brings the rain,
Water runs down your windowpane.

In March spring is very near,
Oh dear, oh dear, oh dear, oh dear.

In April it's my birthday
And Easter, well what can I say?

May brings hot and sunny weather,
Mates play outside together.

In June summer is finally here,
Lots of children cheer.

July brings even more nice weather,
Kids are unlucky the sun's not here forever.

In August the trees have no more leaves
And that is when I start wearing long sleeves.

In September it's my mam's birthday,
This time I am sure I can think of something to say.

October brings Hallowe'en with lots of scary things,
That is what October brings.

November brings Bonfire Night,
If you get hit by a firework it will not be a nice sight.

In December children have a big smile,
When they see their presents in a big pile.

Kaysha Leiah Smith (9)
Carlton Road J&I School

January To December

January brings lots of cheer
As we look forward to a new year.

February brings the snow
Makes our toes and fingers glow.

March brings the Easter bunny,
He is so bouncy and so funny.

April brings the spring
Makes our birds come out and sing.

May is a time for fun
To have a very tasty bun.

June brings out the sun
So people can have lots of fun.

July brings the beers
So people can say *cheers!*

August brings the late nights
So people can have water fights.

September makes leaves fall
While everybody plays football.

October brings all the rain
So people fall over in pain.

November brings Bonfire Night,
All the fireworks are so bright.

December brings Christmas cheer
Now we start a new year.

Victoria Jade Sheppard (10)
Carlton Road J&I School

January To December

January brings lots of cheer
As we look forward to a brand new year.

February brings the snow
But we have a warm place to go.

March brings the rainfall
As I slip into each wall.

April brings out the sun
Me and my dad have lots of fun.

May brings the fierce wind
The tent has to be pinned.

June brings my birthday
I think I'll have a very fun day.

July brings the hailstone
It crashes into the window.

August brings the bad weather
I wear my coat for it is leather.

October brings on the fog
Now we have to find the dog.

November brings the fireworks
I watch them while my dad works.

December brings Christmas
And I hope people have a good Christmas.

Dominic Yates (9)
Carlton Road J&I School

January To December

January brings lots of cheer
As we look forward to a brand new year
February brings the snow
Wild cats don't have a warm place to go
March brings the rain
It's a bad time for aeroplanes
April brings the sun
I have lots of fun
May brings the wind
The tents have to be pinned
June brings the shining sun
Me and my dad have lots of fun
July brings the hailstones
Crashing from window to window
August brings bad weather
Me and my family stay together
September brings the fog
I can't find my dog
October brings my birthday
Then I'll have a fun day
November brings the fireworks
I watch them while my dad works
December brings Christmas
And I really hope everyone has a merry Christmas.

Daniel Hugill (10)
Carlton Road J&I School

My Teacher

My teacher gives us homework
My teacher sings
My teacher is a pain
Because I don't want to work
My teacher is good
Only sometimes
My teacher is the best
My teacher shouts
My teacher squeals
My teacher.

Luke Malone (9)
Carlton Road J&I School

Stop! Are You Thinking?

When you are being racist
Just to show off!
    Stop! Are you thinking?

When you hurt somebody
Inside and out!
    Stop! Are you thinking?

When you tease somebody
Because of their religion!
    Stop! Are you thinking?

When you are being a bully
Because something's gone wrong!
    Stop! Are you thinking?

Now!

Amy Edgley (10)
Farsley Springbank Junior School

I Love To Dance

I love to dance,
To jump and prance,
Every day I have a better chance.

When I do,
I feel as blue,
As the beautiful sky above the moon.

My friends like to dance with me,
As good as S Club 8 we'd like to be,
Then once someone broke her knee.

Our mums like to watch us,
Even if we're on the bus,
They always make a big fuss.

I love to dance,
To jump and prance,
I'd love to do a competition in France.

Olivia Louise Platt (9)
Farsley Springbank Junior School

Dreams

Dreams are a wonderful thing,
They make me want to sing,
All the people that I meet,
Say, 'Take a seat,'
Then I see some animals,
And some boys and gals,
Let's see an elephant squirt water,
Then a pig that's a snorter,
I see a flower then I lean,
Then I realise it's all a dream.

Stephanie Lacey (9)
Farsley Springbank Junior School

Kate Who Picked Her Nose

(Kate who always picked her nose
Got her finger stuck up it!)

Kate picked and picked through the night,
She picked and picked with all her might,
Kate did this and she didn't care,
And ended up with it up there.

Megan Atack (10)
Farsley Springbank Junior School

Bethany Swung On Her Chair And Ended Up With A Broken Back

Bethany swung on her chair,
She'd look at people and would stare,
Today she fell and heard a crack,
Oh dear she had a broken back!

Christina Lang (9)
Farsley Springbank Junior School

Nicole The Niker

Nicole nicked the reading books,
She did all of the dirty looks,
She frightened the teacher to death,
She killed herself by her bad breath.

Amy Ann Sutcliffe (9)
Farsley Springbank Junior School

What's That Noise?

What's that noise?
I hear someone crying,
What's that noise?
Is it a dog howling or
Is it the wind?
What's that noise?
Three loud bangs,
Could it be a
Firework or what?
What's that noise?
I can hear a teacher
Shouting
What a bad boy!

Lucy Hall (9)
Farsley Springbank Junior School

Up Through The Stream

Up through the stream,
I see a bright blue crystal
Shimmering stream and
Up above me, there's
Little bees and birds and
Magnificent, beautiful
Blossoming trees which
Have pink and purple
Cute little buds, up on
The tall trees with
Big, bushy, brown, green
And red leaves.

Megan Harrison (9)
Farsley Springbank Junior School

Me, My Friends And I

Me, my friends and I,
Sing together all the time,
Jump and dance,
Leap and prance.

Do the cat walk,
Then have a little talk,
Our favourite colour is pink,
To make the boys wink.

We gallop like a unicorn,
And skip at the morning dawn,
Brush our hair 100 times,
Put make-up on nearly all the time.

Caitlin Louise McCafferty (10)
Farsley Springbank Junior School

Kira The Girl Who Chattered And Ended Up Not Being Able To Talk

Kira chattered far too much,
She chattered about such and such,
She opened her mouth wide to shout,
However, no more sound came out!

Bethany Shaw (9)
Farsley Springbank Junior School

Spirit Soar

(In memory of Stephen Lawrence)

Let his spirit soar through the midnight air,
Let him fly towards the moon.

In the daylight and the evening,
He shall be forgotten, but not soon.

Richard Thomas Whitley-Peden (9)
Farsley Springbank Junior School

Beth

(Who ate lots and lots and
As a result died eating a cat.)

Beth ate anything she saw,
She even ate off the floor,
She nearly ate a boy's large hat,
And died eating a fluffy cat.

Abby Coates (9)
Farsley Springbank Junior School

Lozi

(Who was very thin and became fat
And as a result she popped.)

Lozi was extremely thin,
But then became like a dustbin,
She ate and ate and could not stop,
Till in the end she did just pop.

Rebecca Donaldson (9)
Farsley Springbank Junior School

Ryan Who Was A Robber And As A Result Got Killed

Ryan was a robber - bad,
Who stole from banks which made cops mad,
One day, from them, he tried to run,
But then they shot him with a gun.

Ryan Rogers (9)
Farsley Springbank Junior School

Seaside

S ee the birds singing in the sky,
E xciting to see the waves high,
A nd I liked the ice cream at the beach,
S ee the beautiful animals in the sea,
I see people enjoying themselves, laughing,
D o the activities and you'll feel great,
E ating the scrummy food.

Rachel Louise Rogers (9)
Farsley Springbank Junior School

Why Does The Wind?

Why does the wind howl like it does?
Why don't the birds sing like us?
Why does the sea roar in tune?
Why doesn't the sun come out with the moon?
What will this world bring next year?
Will it be different every year . . .

Nicole Bramley (10)
Farsley Springbank Junior School

Jack

(Who thought he was the best and
As a result committed suicide.)

Jack who thought he was the best,
And collected things in his vest,
Until one day he found a cane,
And whacked himself and died in pain.

Karl Morris (9)
Farsley Springbank Junior School

John Who Was A Very Bad Lad

(As a result got put in jail
And sliced himself to death.)

John was a naughty lad,
Who took the mick out of his fat dad
He also went round hitting folk
Until he said a stupid joke
Then one day found himself banged up,
And cut himself with a glass cup.

Adam Swales (9)
Farsley Springbank Junior School

Amy Who Always Sucked Her Thumb

(Amy always sucked her thumb and
As a result died painfully.)

Amy always sucked her thumb,
And then got told off by her mum,
She sucked so much the flesh off came
And then she died of awful pain.

Bethany Grace Gaunt (10)
Farsley Springbank Junior School

Lewis Who Had No Friends

(Lewis who had no friends as a result was lonely.)

Lewis who was so unkind,
Was always playing with kid's minds,
A bigger boy whom he did push,
Killed him with one violent crush.

Lewis James Thornton (10)
Farsley Springbank Junior School

Lewis

(Who ate and ate and as
A result got in trouble.)

Lewis was a greedy lad,
Who one day was so very bad,
He opened up the biscuit tin,
His mum found out and shoved him in,
And now he lives within the tin,
His food went in the dusty bin,
He died of starvation poor knave
And now he lives deep in his grave.

Emma Jennings (10)
Farsley Springbank Junior School

Anger

Anger is crimson,
It smells like fire,
It tastes like burnt jelly,
It sounds like people biting their food,
It feels like someone sweating,
It lives in your fist.

Megan Paige Reed (9)
Farsley Springbank Junior School

Health

The colour of health is apple-green,
Health smells like fresh fruit,
It tastes like honey and bread,
Health sounds like soft music playing,
It feels like fluffy pillows,
Health lives high in the clouds!

Olivia Mary Taylor (10)
Farsley Springbank Junior School

Ben

(Who picked his nose till he fell to bits.)

Ben did always pick his nose,
Sometimes his nostrils would not close,
He picked his nose with this and that,
Sometimes he used a cricket bat,
His manners were extremely bad,
People called him manky lad,
He only lived 'til he was six,
When suddenly he fell to bits.

Bethany Broadbent (10)
Farsley Springbank Junior School

Tommy

(Who ate and ate
And as a result he exploded.)

Tommy was a greedy kid,
He even ate his hamster Sid,
Finally he ate too much,
When he popped out came his dog Butch.

Jamie Mark Kemp (9)
Farsley Springbank Junior School

Jake

(Who ate until he choked.)

Jake he was a greedy kid,
Who ate and ate the treats he'd hid,
One day when he was in his room,
He choked on ham and fell to doom.

Joe Firth (10)
Farsley Springbank Junior School

Lewis

(Who grassed and
Got the Maphias cross.)

Lewis liked to grass a lot
He saw the Maphias secret plot
He kept it quiet for one whole week
But then he had to have one more peek,
He went back one bright summer's day
And this is what the Mob did say
'Tell the cops and you will slay,'
He ran off as scared as can be,
To go tell the authorities
The Mob ran after him real fast,
And killed that foolish grass at last.

Joseph Pritchard (9)
Farsley Springbank Junior School

Steph

(Who was a greedy kid
And as a result died whilst being sick.)

Steph was such a greedy kid,
Who ate and ate and drank fluid,
She fattened up like a huge ball,
And down the stairs she had a fall,
At first she shrieked a painful scream,
When came in her dad's footie team,
They called the ambulance dead quick,
But Steph, she died whilst being sick.

Ami Cookes (9)
Farsley Springbank Junior School

Joe Who Was A Greedy Boy

(Who was a greedy boy
And as a result choked to death.)

Joe was a greedy boy,
Who even ate his blue car toy,
But then he ate his bedroom door,
And ended up dead on the floor.

Amy Smith (10)
Farsley Springbank Junior School

Emma

(Who ate too much and
As a result exploded.)

Emma was a greedy kid,
She always opened biscuit lids,
She ate pizza and burgers first,
But after cake, she finally burst.

Lauren Newstead (9)
Farsley Springbank Junior School

Emma

(Who ate until
Her body collapsed.)

Emma was a greedy kid,
Who always opened cookie lids,
She often got away with it
Until one day she fell to bits.

Bethany Stanbridge (10)
Farsley Springbank Junior School

John Who Stuck His Tongue Out!

(Who stuck his tongue out
And ended up not being able
To get it in again.)

John who always stuck his tongue out wide,
He could not put it back inside,
He tried and tried to put it back,
He ended up with a heart attack.

Sam Brayshaw (9)
Farsley Springbank Junior School

Happiness

Happiness is light blue,
It smells like a big blue lollipop,
It tastes like a big, juicy melon in a smiley shape,
It sounds like a little baby laughing,
It feels like a soft, smooth, silk blanket,
It lives around everyone.

Amelia Lumb (9)
Farsley Springbank Junior School

George

(Who ate and ate until he burst.)

George who was a greedy kid,
Who ate and ate the cakes Mum hid,
He found the lot and scoffed them all,
Until he burst just like a ball!

George Hardaker (10)
Farsley Springbank Junior School

Are You My Friend?

I may not always show it,
But you know that I care,
Whenever you need me,
You know I'll be there.

Your happiness makes me smile,
I am glad you're my friend,
Knowing that you're my pal,
Will bring me joy to the end.

It's impossible to recollect,
The 'Do you remember the time when?'
And no calculator could add up
All the times we've exchanged grins.

I hope you never change,
How wonderful you are,
You and I forever,
Is my wish beyond a star.

Ella Park (9)
Farsley Springbank Junior School

Happiness Is . . .

Happiness is having a smile on your face,
Happiness is being with your friends playing chase,
Happiness is love in your own heart,
Happiness is a special kind of art,
Happiness is getting something you love,
Happiness is a sign from above,
Happiness is beautiful,
Happiness is never dull,
Happiness is all around the universe,
And this is the end of my very last verse.

Laura Sereena Chawla (10)
Farsley Springbank Junior School

Beauty In The Countryside

In the lovely countryside a beauty comes with swift,
Everybody around the town comes to see this sight,
All the people crowd around the beauty being born,
Suddenly, suddenly the beauty is a tiny flower
Everything around the flower gives life force and power.

For centuries and centuries the flower starts to grow,
So the plant gives the town a happy, cheerful glow,
The glow fades, the town is dark,
Then the town's people start to shout,
'Oh please, oh please great big flower,
Shine on our dark, damp town and
We'll give you more power.'

Carl Place (9)
Farsley Springbank Junior School

Bird Of Time

Time is like a bird
Soaring through the sky,
Quicker and quicker, time is passing by,
Time is passing by just like the morning bird,
But just like time, it is never heard.
The garden hopper is passing by,
Just like the morning sky,
Time can race straight past you like a bird soaring by,
Time is always there, just like the morning sky,
Time is passing by, never to be seen again,
Just like a bird that will never be seen again.

Ryan Olliver (9)
Farsley Springbank Junior School

Foxes

Rabbit eater,
Chicken chaser,
Meat carrier,
Grouchy growler,
Family feeder,
Family fetcher.

Lauren Hammill (9)
Horbury Bridge CE J&I Primary School

My Dog Molly

She is a bone licker,
Fast runner,
Ball chaser,
Meat eater,
Good dog Molly.

Kelsey Verity (9)
Horbury Bridge CE J&I Primary School

Cars

C ars are cool and good looking
A nd they're fast and smooth.
R aging motors in the back of them,
S mall but great brass wheels.

Connor Gosnay (8)
Horbury Bridge CE J&I Primary School

Bugs

If I were a bug I'd be slimy,
My coat would be black and shiny.
I'd climb up high and touch the sky
And always be happy and smiley.

Victoria Wilson (7)
Horbury Bridge CE J&I Primary School

Sharks

S harp, sparkling, white teeth,
H uman beings ripped to pieces.
A great killing machine,
R aising huge jaws above water,
K illing at will,
S harks are deadly creatures.

Ben Terry (7)
Horbury Bridge CE J&I Primary School

Grass

Grass is green but is never seen
In town and city streets.
We take for granted
What is planted.
Some other people may never have seen.

Lucy Tolson (8)
Horbury Bridge CE J&I Primary School

Stars

S hiny figures in the sky,
T winkling stars at night.
A bove the world in space, stars will be there,
R unning slowly in the sky.

Luke Rogerson (7)
Horbury Bridge CE J&I Primary School

Star

S pecial little dots in the sky.
T winkling brightly, shining high.
A lways ready to shine.
R eady to grant wishes at any time.

Hollie Senior (8)
Horbury Bridge CE J&I Primary School

Man Utd

Man Utd are my favourite team,
They are captained by Roy Keane.

They pass the ball with flair and skill
Especially brothers Gary and Phil.

They really know how to score a goal
But I still miss Andy Cole.

They score lots of good goals
With my favourite, Paul Scholes.

The opposing defender looks like a boy
When the ball is with van Nistelrooy.

We won the double in '94 and '96
With the help of our ace, Ryan Giggs.

The opposing striker is a coward
When faced with our keeper, Tim Howard.

Real Madrid look like Huddersfield Town
When challenged by the mighty Wes Brown.

Losing with 2 minutes to go, to lose would be folly,
But first it was Sheringham, then thank goodness for Ole.

European, FA Cup, Premier League, that was fine,
Oh what a year was 1999!

Jack Lonsdale (8)
Horbury Bridge CE J&I Primary School

Dancing

I have a friend called Sally,
I know her because we both go to ballet.
We point our toes down
And dance round and round
And curtsey to Madame O'Malley.

Megan Schofield (7)
Horbury Bridge CE J&I Primary School

Fairy Folk

Fairies are tiny things,
Able to fly using delicate wings.
They spread their love everywhere,
Just to show how much they care.

Leprechauns are sneaky,
They're usually very cheeky.
It'll cause havoc in your home,
Will this mischievous little gnome.

Goblins are green,
But hardly ever seen.
They have very pointy chins
And sneaky little grins.

Elves work hard every day,
They never get a chance to play.
Helpful to have around,
Working hard, not making a sound.

So now you know,
This is no joke,
The mysterious lives
Of our fairy folk.

Millie Fowles (8)
Horbury Bridge CE J&I Primary School

Night-Time

When I go to bed, night-time comes.
When I am in bed I hear the owls hoot,
But then I hear foxes howling as they wake me up.
Hedgehogs come out to see their furry friends,
Then the bats, the black and gloomy bats.
When morning comes I open my eyes
And see the daylight appear.

Claire Crow (9)
Horbury Bridge CE J&I Primary School

Cleaning My Bedroom

Cleaning my bedroom,
Oh what a pain,
To me it looks tidy
So I'm not to blame.
I like my toys on the floor,
Not behind a cupboard door.

Thomas Barber (9)
Horbury Bridge CE J&I Primary School

Cleaning My Bedroom

Toys here, toys there,
Toys everywhere,
Put some here,
Put some there,
Let's hide my favourite toy behind there.

Jason Barber (8)
Horbury Bridge CE J&I Primary School

My Family And Me

I love my mum
And she loves me
And with my dad
That makes three.

Olivia Allott (7)
Horbury Bridge CE J&I Primary School

Doodles

Doodles is a friendly bunny,
He performs tricks which are very funny.
He races around the garden like crazy,
Sometimes he is very lazy.
He gobbles his food down like a hog,
He used to play with my grandma's dog.
He is loveable all the time,
I am glad that he is mine!

Nikki Lonsdale (9)
Horbury Bridge CE J&I Primary School

Fractions

Fractions are hard,
Fractions are bad,
Multiplying them,
Adding them,
Taking them away,
Fractions drive me mad!

Eleanor Mitchell (10)
Horbury Bridge CE J&I Primary School

Tudors

T here was a fat king called Henry,
U nder the roof of pure royalty,
D ied an unpleasant death,
O vertaken by Ed,
R uled for a bit,
S oon the women took over!

Bradley Gearey (10)
Horbury Bridge CE J&I Primary School

Good Charlotte

G oths,
O ffspring,
O ddity,
D rums.

C rashing shops,
H ating the world,
A narchy,
R ock and roll,
L inkin' Park,
O ver the top,
T aking over,
T rashing everything,
E lectric guitars.

Damian Brayshaw (11)
Horbury Bridge CE J&I Primary School

Joe The Menace

Joe was a menace
Who lived in Venice.
He once got caught by the police
For planting a bomb in Greece,
But he dug and dug, then dug himself out,
He went undercover and started sneaking about,
So every night, lock your door,
Otherwise he'll start stealing just like before.

Herbie Naylor Mayers (11)
Horbury Bridge CE J&I Primary School

Teachers

T errific,
E legant,
A mazing,
C unning,
H appy,
E xciting,
R ich,
S uper.

Ryan Verity (10)
Horbury Bridge CE J&I Primary School

Christmas Eve

Santa coming on his way,
With mince pies and sherry he'd love to stay,
He's dropping off presents for girls and boys,
Hoping they will love their toys,
But he must hurry up and leave,
This December on Christmas Eve.

Amy Cudworth (11)
Horbury Bridge CE J&I Primary School

SATs

S candalous spelling
A venging English
T errible maths
S uicidal science.

Argh!

Jamie Lamont (11)
Horbury Bridge CE J&I Primary School

Mary Had A Little Lamb

Mary had a little lamb,
Its boots were made of leather,
It followed her to school one day
And made it rain bad weather.

Mary had a little lamb,
Its fleece was white of course,
It followed her to school one day
And everybody shouted, 'Mint sauce.'

Mary had a little lamb,
Its cheeks were covered in blusher,
It followed her to school one day,
But they decided to go to Russia.

Mary had a little lamb,
Its fleece was black as coal,
It followed her into space one day
And fell down a great big black hole.

Natalie Cudworth (9)
Horbury Bridge CE J&I Primary School

My Puppy Lucy

My puppy Lucy is very small,
She likes to play with her ball.
She likes to run and have some fun,
She likes to fight and bite.
She is fast,
I am last.

Matthew Evans (10)
Horbury Bridge CE J&I Primary School

A River's Life

Twisting, winding, whirling,
Bobbing up and down.
Smashing, crashing, swirling,
Flowing all around.

The river has all flooded,
The banks cannot be seen,
Houses covered with water,
Higher than you and me.

Twisting, winding, whirling,
Soaking the flood plain.
Smashing, crashing, swirling,
It's a river's life again.

Ellis Birkby (10)
Inglebrook School

The River

Water trickles down the hill,
At this point the water is still.
The water keeps flowing, not much it will carry,
Then finally it reaches it tributary.
It keeps getting bigger and bigger and bigger
And then it starts to form its figure.
Then it flows, crashing and dancing and splashing,
It gets much rougher, then it fiercely starts lashing.
It meanders round fields but still flows on,
It goes and goes, it is never gone.
It follows its course down to the sea
And at last it finishes at the estuary.

Ashleigh Brain (10)
Inglebrook School

From A Babbling Brook

Its source is at the top of a mountain,
Water is pouring like a fountain.
From its water lots of animals drink.
If it decided to be choppy lots of boats sink.
Lapping softly it can sometimes be,
Gentle, still and a lot like me.
But a lot of the time it decides to go crashing,
Houses are flooding and ferries are smashing.
I've forgotten how many treetops have gone,
Each has vanished. Every one!

Whirling and swirling it goes to the sea,
At its estuary it takes the shape of a B.
Sometimes when things are not quite right,
You fall in it more than once in the light!
You go back home dripping wet
And your mum says, 'Don't be upset.'
She thinks it's tears that are on your face,
Trickling down like it's a race.
So when you're there don't forget to look
At the swirling, whirling, babbling brook.

Lucy Fox (10)
Inglebrook School

A River

A river goes to the sea
Meeting people like you and me.
It carries pebbles all the way,
Depositing them somewhere else some day.
The river starts to twist and turn
When it's joined by a burn.
Then the river joins the sea,
Passing people like you and me.

Thomas Copley (10)
Inglebrook School

Water, Water

Water, water trickling around,
Gushing and swaying as it goes down.
Splashing and crashing as it goes,
Freezing cold for our toes.
Fishes and frogs swim about,
Never bothering to get out.
Water makes things turn to mud,
Sometimes even makes a flood.
Water never stays still,
Trickling and falling down the hill.

James Harrison (9)
Inglebrook School

The River

Crashing, bashing down the stream,
Gleaming in the sun.
Shallow and deep the river is,
A place for swimming and fun.

Light and dark is the river flowing,
It ends its journey at the sea.
But still the water keeps on going,
Rivers never end you see.

Rachel Connell (10)
Inglebrook School

The River

The river goes fast and slow
But for how long does it go?
The river is deep, the river is shallow,
Through the gorge it's flowing narrow.

Ashley Elliott (10)
Inglebrook School

The River

One day I was in a boat
When I came up to a lock.
I went in and out,
The water swirled about,
When I looked, I found
I was in Fairyland.

So I sailed with the current
Until I was back on earth.
Then I saw the water flow,
It was bending like a meander.
Then I hit a rock
And I was overboard.

Lewis Waring (9)
Inglebrook School

The River Slide

Water crashes against the rocks
And whirls and ripples around,
The level rises and the houses flood
As the water covers the ground.

The water splashes and pours over the banks
And twists through the countryside
Eroding the rocks, the water falls
Through the mountains like a slide.

Michael Ellis (9)
Inglebrook School

Ginger The Horse

Ginger likes her hay,
She will chew on it all day.
She goes out to play nice and clean,
She comes back in all muddy and green.

Hadley Stringer (11)
Inglebrook School

Alfie My Pup

A lfie is a puppy dog,
L eft and right he runs around,
F unny little chap he is,
I love him lots because he's mine,
E ither way he's the best.

M y mum says he's a real mess,
Y es sometimes I do agree.

P layful my puppy is
U nless he's hungry,
P ick him up and put him to bed.

Sophie Astle (11)
Inglebrook School

Desert

The hot barren desert
Has not seen water for weeks.
The few people who live there struggle
But the snake slithering slowly
Thrives, finding rock and grass
To shelter from the heat of the sun.

Andrew Earnshaw (10)
Inglebrook School

The River

Rocks eroded and rivers flow,
Winding joyfully as they go
And the creatures down below
Look for food to help them grow.

Amrit Bance (10)
Inglebrook School

Food

My favourite food is beef,
The bits get stuck in my teeth.
You have to use a cocktail stick
To have a little pick.

My other favourite food is curry,
You have to eat it in a hurry.
Vindaloo is the hottest of them all,
It's so hot you might trip and fall.

My least favourite food is mushy peas,
They always make me sneeze!
Now I have told you about my favourite foods,
I'm going to go off in a mood.

Alice Sandham (10)
Inglebrook School

My Brother

My brother never does as he is told
And he always says, 'I'm bold.'
I call him bossy,
He calls me mossy.
He chases the dog
And jumps over logs.
His name is Adam Lewis Cook,
But he always has bad luck.
Then again I have to admit
I won't get anyone better than him.
So I guess he's the best brother ever.

Rachel Cook (10)
Inglebrook School

The River Severn

The River Severn
Winds and twists,
A muddy river bank
Or a boat that's probably sunk,
With a bridge here and there,
Sand on the bottom
And land everywhere.

Laura Pindar (10)
Inglebrook School

Storm

Storm, a stressed adult,
Letting its anger out on the world.
Nobody to turn to 'cause nobody cares,
For the sad and lonely storm.

He growls and grumbles,
Twisting and turning through the sky.
Throwing his friends, on objects he spies.
Until at last the rain shimmers down
And then the storm dies away until another day.
He's scared of the rain, so he hides behind a cloud,
A fluffy white cloud.

Hannah Shields (11)
Manston St James Primary School

Tabby Cat - Cinquain

A cat
Has gone missing
From a home in England
It is a stripy tabby cat
Please help!

Rachel MacFadyen (10)
Manston St James Primary School

The Children In My Class

The children in my class are very annoying,
They're as thick as thumb,
Just like my mum.
They dance on the table, they swing on the light,
When teacher walks in they sure give her a fright.

They don't know how to dance and can't even sing,
They can't spell, they don't know anything.
They can't count to twenty not even to four,
All they can do is cartwheel round the floor.

You should see them in the dining hall, they eat like a bear,
They put jelly on the sarnies, put chocolate in their hair.
Looby is the worst not forgetting Ted
And as for Mark and Leo they dance on my head.

Why I'm in their class I really do not know,
Perhaps it's the fact I have a great big toe.
Maybe they're silly because they're three years old
And I'm nearly eleven as I've been told.

Maybe there was a mix-up as we walked around the schools,
I blame the teachers, they're silly old fools.
I can't blame the children, they're not even five
And I suppose after all they are alive.

They keep me in this class because I'm so small,
Oh my golly gosh do I wish I was tall.
I've told the teachers I'm ten years of age,
But they just ignore me as I'm locked up in a cage.

Oh I can't say much more, I'm getting too tired,
So please help me out and get these teachers . . . fired!

Rachael Kennedy (10)
Manston St James Primary School

Where Is A Friend When You Need One?

Where is a friend when you need one?
Where is a friend to play?
Where is a friend to shine like the sun on a rainy day?
Where is a friend when you need one?

Where is a friend when you're lonely?
Where is a friend when you're sad?
Where is a friend to calm you down when you're angry and mad?
Where is a friend when you need one?

Where is a friend to share?
Where is a friend to stand beside you?
Where is a friend to care?
Where is a friend when you need one?

Rebecca Hardy (11)
Manston St James Primary School

The Swimming Pool

I like swimming in the pool,
I like the way it makes me float,
I like feeling free like a big fish,
Hey that would be really cool.

Underwater is a whole new world
With tropical fish and mermaids.
I'd like to think there was a magical world
Where there was no war, hurt or pain.
When I swim underwater, I can't hear any sound
Like all the fighting in this world on Earth's rocky ground.

Jayshree Chudasama (11)
Manston St James Primary School

Air - Cinquain

Blue sky
Gold dot of flame
Fluff floating in the sky
Wind howling, a swirling blizzard
Thunder.

Dominic Martill (10)
Menston Primary School

The Snowflake - Cinquain

White, small
Patterned snowflake,
Falls onto the still world.
Children play in the cold, white sheet
It leaves.

Alice Harrison & Megan Smith (10)
Menston Primary School

Cinquains Have - Cinquain

Cinquains
Have five lines and
Its syllable pattern
Is two, four, six, eight, two and they're
Diffic . . .

Jacob Bentley (10)
Menston Primary School

Painless - Cinquain

Silence . . .
Soft snowflakes drift
Causing a white blanket,
Smothering the cruel, painful world,
Silence . . .

Hannah Hartley (11)
Menston Primary School

Tranquillity - Cinquain

Silence . . .
Icicles hang,
Frozen waters lie still,
Ice fully engulfs the huge world,
Silence . . .

Adam Dinsdale (11)
Menston Primary School

Lunchtime - Cinquain

Lunchtime,
No more hunger,
The big rush to the line,
Then eating, eating, there's no noise,
Next . . . tea!

Samuel Akroyd (10)
Menston Primary School

Easy Death - Cinquain

Just there . . .
The deep blue moon . . .
Howling, blowing wind. Stop,
All around silence fills the land
Still. Death . . .

Bethany Sunderland (11)
Menston Primary School

Midnight - Cinquain

Midnight,
I am alone,
With the moon and the stars,
The wolf is near, he howls at me.
Goodbye.

Hannah Montague-Millar & Olivia Winter (10)
Menston Primary School

All Around - Cinquain

Watch here
What do you see?
Leaves falling on the ground,
Crisp, red leaves, conkers are prickly,
Autumn.

Alex Bowman (10)
Menston Primary School

Dawn - Cinquain

Silence.
A lone bird sings,
Leaves rustle in the wind,
Everyone is asleep, until:
Light comes.

Katie Bailey & Ruth Hobley (10)
Menston Primary School

The Season - Cinquain

Footsteps
Into the shade,
Slurping on cold ice cream,
No breeze at all, nothing but sun,
Summer!

Mercedes Green (11)
Menston Primary School

Tears - Cinquain

Christmas
Presents open,
Then tear by tear by tear,
Why are there tears by people in
Themselves?

William Betts (10)
Menston Primary School

A Bouncing Bunny

A hopping hopper,
A high hopper,
A padded pouch
Where the youngsters crouch,
Light brown,
Fluffy and furry.

    A
        catalogue
                to
                      make
                            me
                                kangaroo.

Nathan Shields & Jordan Bentley (10)
Menston Primary School

Squiggly Wiggly

A very squiggly
Long and wiggly.

Fangs of venom
Poison from.

Rattle and hiss
Hope you miss.

Quick, quick, quick
A slick,
A catalogue to make me snake.

Ellie English (11)
Menston Primary School

A Vicious Snap

A nipping claw,
A pinching pesk.

A scuttling pain,
A crispy shell.

A bad temper,
A roaring attitude.

A catalogue to make me crab.

Eleanor Midgley & Lana Hutton (10)
Menston Primary School

Large Fowl

A long neck,
A pecky beak.

A plump body,
Big eggs.

Thin legs,
Large strides.

A catalogue to make me an ostrich.

Emily Cooper & Lisa Emsley (10)
Menston Primary School

Nightfall - Cinquain

Hunting
An animal
It stalks, looking for food,
A wolf. It howls in great sadness
Listening.

Lauren Scaife (11)
Menston Primary School

A Grass Eater

A long neck,
Long legs.

A smooth skin,
Small feet.

A long tail,
A tartan coat.

A catalogue to make me giraffe.

Yuqing Jiang & David Ratcliffe (10)
Menston Primary School

Diving Dipper

A fast fisher,
A fish wisher.

A diving dipper,
A flying whipper.

A colour flash,
Splash, splash, splash.

A catalogue to make me kingfisher.

Ross Hammond (11)
Menston Primary School

The Stars

I am a star in the dark night sky,
I sleep all day, play all night.
When I pop into view shadows wake up
And dance the night right through.

Calum Miller (8)
Roberttown J&I CE (C) School

The Giant Green Monster

Once upon a time I went to school and saw a monster.
Once upon a time I went to school and saw a green monster.
Once upon a time I went to school and saw a green, sapphire monster.
Once upon a time I went to school and saw a green, sapphire, ugly monster.
Once upon a time I went to school and saw a green, sapphire, ugly, slimy monster.
Once upon a time I went to school and saw a green, sapphire, ugly, slimy, inky monster.
Once upon a time I went to school and saw a green, sapphire, ugly, slimy, inky, rat-infested monster.
Once upon a time I went to school and saw a green, sapphire, ugly, slimy, inky, rat-infested, spiky monster.
Once upon a time I went to school and saw a green, sapphire, ugly, slimy, inky, rat-infested, spiky, mad monster
 . . . on the road.

Joseph Kerr (8)
Roberttown J&I CE (C) School

I Wake Up

I wake up,
I cannot see,
I feel like I am not me.
I try and struggle out of bed,
'There's no point,' I said.
I close my eyes once again,
I wriggle but I don't have any pain.
It lasts for one blink or two
And then it disappears into thin air
And there's no shadow or a stare!

Bethany Ruston (9)
Roberttown J&I CE (C) School

What Is . . . ?

What's a face without a smile?
What's a wait without a while?
What's a push without a shove?
What's a hug without any love?

What's a letter without the words?
What's a sky without the birds?
What's a night without the moon?
What's a song without a tune?

What's a clock without the time?
What's a ruler without a line?
What's a candle without a flame?
What's a person without a name?

What's a flower without a petal?
What's the snow if it doesn't settle?
What's a dance without a dancer?
What's a question without an answer?

Hannah Mather (10)
Roberttown J&I CE (C) School

Early Morning

As the Earth awakes
To see the wonderful lakes.

The distant blue lagoon,
Tourists saying, 'See you soon.'

The beautiful blue sky
Later to turn to night.

A sight for sore eyes,
The wildlife full of butterflies.

People leaving the shoreline,
Going to dine.

Thomas Dixon (11)
Roberttown J&I CE (C) School

The Exam

*Butterflies dance the tango
Whilst on my way to the exam.*

Stuck in traffic all day long,
Wet and drippy, all full of cold.

Get to the church all tired and hungry,
'I wonder if they'll have some buns?'

*Butterflies dance the tango
Whilst on my way to the exam.*

The church is big with a steeple,
Pointy enough to touch the sky.

Walk through the big and wooden doors
Holding my dad's big, warm hand.

*Butterflies dance the tango
Whilst on my way to the exam.*

My name is suddenly shouted,
I spring up from the chair.

Through the creaky doors I go
And look on in despair.

*Butterflies dance the tango
Whilst on my way to the exam.*

I am the first to go in
And I do my very best.

I play the piano carefully,
Then look into the air.

*Butterflies dance the tango
Whilst on my way to the exam.*

. . . . All you can do is your best!

Charlotte Glaves (8)
Roberttown J&I CE (C) School

Midnight

In the woods, all alone,
Lightning strikes, midnight.

Wolves crying with hunger,
Moonlight shining down.

Blindfolded by darkness,
The demons haunting.

Witches on their broomsticks,
Flying through the night.

In the woods on Hallowe'en,
Midnight!

Jessica Mott (11)
Roberttown J&I CE (C) School

The Stars

The stars are twinkling,
The stars are bright,
They dangle down on my bright blue eyes.
I see a star in the sky telling me to go left and right,
I fly high in the sky,
Before I reach them they say bye.

Chloe Armitage (8)
Roberttown J&I CE (C) School

Friendship

Friendship is a candle that will never burn out,
A mountain that will never break away,
A shooting star that will last forever,
A dream that will go on and on,
That's what friendship is.

Amy Peacock (9)
Roberttown J&I CE (C) School

Life

Life's like hanging from a thread,
Just because you're getting ahead
Doesn't mean your life is perfect,
You have got to earn respect,
Things aren't easy,
Things aren't easy.

Take what you have and don't let go,
Understand when people say no,
Things aren't always going to be good,
Even if you don't try and say you understood,
Things aren't easy,
Things aren't easy.

When your life is coming to an end,
Just remember you can't mend
All the bad things in your life,
All the pain and all the strife,
Things aren't easy,
Things aren't easy.

Josef Balach (11)
Roberttown J&I CE (C) School

Amazing Earth

Earth is a giant ball floating through the darkness of space.
It makes all that's dark light as it floats through the darkness.
It destroys anything in its path as it floats through the darkness.
The blue of the sea glows in the darkness of space.
The yellow of the desert shines with glee in the darkness.
The green of the forest keeps all in place in the darkness.
Amazing Earth amazes me.

Ben Tillotson (10)
Roberttown J&I CE (C) School

Mount Kilimanjaro

Dark is the mountain's colour,
No snow, no ice,
The mountain's getting fuller,
But at what price?

Mountaineers climbing up,
Puffing and panting,
Equipment getting heavier,
Slipping and prancing.

Mountaineers reach the top,
No trouble, no shame,
Shouting that they've got to the top,
But won't go up again.

Lexy Clavin (10)
Roberttown J&I CE (C) School

If I Won The Lottery!

If I won the lottery
I would buy a pink metallic sports car
And a huge Cadbury's chocolate bar.
If I won the lottery
I would go shopping every day
And everyone would be happy and gay.
If I won the lottery
I would buy a gigantic luxury mansion
And start a new fashion.
If I won the lottery
I would buy pink silky curtains
And climb some snowy mountains.
If I won the lottery . . .

Shelby Hutchison & Abigail Binns (10)
Roberttown J&I CE (C) School

How Doth The Little Elephant

How doth the little elephant
Improve his swinging tail?
It swings so fast it knocks the ant
Into the great big gale.

How fishy he seems to laugh,
How gently he spreads his teeth
And proudly makes their bath
And eats them with relief.

Melissa Wallis (9)
Roberttown J&I CE (C) School

Your Finest Hour

'And when he gets to Heaven
To Saint Peter he will tell
One more soldier reporting Sir,
I've served my time in Hell'.

Remember the days when they were all strong.
Remember the days when they were never wrong.
Remember the days they fought the enemy.
Remember the days they brought peace to the Earth
And brought down the elimination of the war machines.

Matthew Stone (10)
Roberttown J&I CE (C) School

What They Are Like

Cloudy days are like a blanket in the sky.
Rainy days are like water dropping from the tap.
Sunny days are like a bright material with a torch inside it.
Snowy days are like a big sheet over the country.
Windy days are like a vacuum cleaning the floor.

Mica Jade Gallagher (10)
Roberttown J&I CE (C) School

Snowy Mountains

The snow-covered mountains
Like a white blanket
On a cold winter's day.

The snow leopard's prowling
Around a poor Hyrax burrow
On a cold winter's day.

The murky mountains
Shrouded in mist
On a cold winter's day.

The trees caked in snow,
A snowy owl watches
On a cold winter's day.

The bright snow
Sparkling in the sun
On a cold winter's day.

The ski run's packed
And the tourists in the cable cars
On a cold winter's day.

The snowy mountain
Rising out of a carpet of trees
On a cold winter's day.

Sam Sessions (11)
Roberttown J&I CE (C) School

I Would Like To . . .

I would like to hear a camouflaged chameleon,
I would like to see in the dark,
I would like to touch sweet bins,
I would like to smell a rough rock,
I would like to taste the cheesy moon,
I would like to . . . !

Andrew Lenk (8)
Roberttown J&I CE (C) School

Midnight

Black is the colour of the night,
Black is the colour of fear.
Black is the colour of thunder,
Black is the colour of midnight.

Grey is the colour of rainclouds,
Grey is the colour of sadness.
Grey is the colour of depression,
Grey is the colour of midnight.

Purple is the colour of kites,
Purple is the colour of bruises.
Purple is the colour of lights,
Purple is the colour of midnight.

Blue is the colour of the sky,
Blue is the colour of the sea.
Blue is the colour of anger,
Blue is the colour of midnight.

Midnight!

Siobhan Brogden (11)
Roberttown J&I CE (C) School

The Jambos

In the land of the Jambos
The Japango tree grows.
The Jambos have lived there for a jazillion years,
The Japango tree follows them wherever they go!

They eat fishes on dishes with sweet cooked salami,
They drink jungle juice on little purple chapattis!
Their looks vary from hairy to scary,
Some are charming but others are alarming!

James Enevoldson (11)
Roberttown J&I CE (C) School

Poem

What is pink?
Pink is my bed
Where I lay down my sweet head.

What is red?
Red is a rose
Tickling my toes.

What is black?
Black is my dad's hair,
But I see him very rarely.

What is blue?
Blue is my rug
That keeps me nice and snug.

What is green?
Green is a bean
But my sister's very mean.

Beth Armson (9)
Roberttown J&I CE (C) School

The Land Of Foola

In the land of Foola
A Mov was born
And the first thing he said was, 'Mama!'

He crawled around on his fifteen hands
And jumped up and down on his tail.
His parents were happy, they smiled with glee.

Alas there was something strange to see!
This poor Mov was born with no eyes,
Look at it now, I tell no lies.

James Sutcliffe (10)
Roberttown J&I CE (C) School

In The Garden

Sizzling sausages burning on the barbecue,
People playing, having lots of fun.
Shoulder carries, piggyback rides,
So much pleasure, so glad to be here.

High spirits shine the day bright,
Brothers and sisters, family and friends
All joined together so the day never ends.
Playing on the swings so high in the sky.

Splashing in the paddling pool,
It is so very cool,
Swirling and twirling all around,
Always end up falling to the ground.

Kerry Brooks (10)
Roberttown J&I CE (C) School

My Mum

She stands under the arbour with bouquet in hand,
In white from head to toe,
Smiling at her mum and dad,
The lace of her dress like a carpet of fresh snow on the ground,
The lingering freshness of summer and autumn leaves on the trees,
The sparkle of the sky like a wave on the beach,
The twisted ivy like a green rope around the arbour,
The tree trunk shimmers in the September sun,
The lushness of the grass like a rug on the ground.

My mum is special,
She's my hero,
I love my mum.

Louisa Binns (11)
Roberttown J&I CE (C) School

On An Autumn Morning

Down the frosty mountains,
Through the really rich grass,
Here you are next to a blue, blue lake
Trickling down the wall.

Boats are always floating,
Trees are swishing fast
Right towards the banking,
Can you feel the breeze?

Alex Shaw (10)
Roberttown J&I CE (C) School

Light Vs Darkness

The clouds of darkness are approaching the light,
It is like a clash of light and dark,
Everyone trying to prevent the force of the shady,
Dark, dismal clouds spoiling the wonderful
Atmosphere of the summer days,
Children playing in the sandpits
And adults watching over them.

Sam Purssell (10)
Roberttown J&I CE (C) School

A Journey Through My Senses . . .

I would like to see the waves in the sky,
I would like to hear the whistling of the birds,
I would like to smell the baking of the bread,
I would like to touch the bumpy, velvety flower,
I want to be happy all the time.

Emmeline Robinson (7)
Roberttown J&I CE (C) School

Nonsense Poem (The Rabbigs)

Far and away, far and away
Is the land where the Rabbigs live,
Their heads are pink and their hands are red
And they never get out of their bed, bed, bed,
They never get out of their bed.

Every day they eat cheese and lots and lots of plates of peas
With ice cream and chips, they have big fat hips.
They wobble around on the pink spotty ground,
Licking some lollies with plenty of dollies,
Is the land where the Rabbigs live.

Far and away, far and away
Is the land where the Rabbigs live,
Their heads are pink and their hands are red
And they never get out of their bed, bed, bed,
They never get out of their bed.

The Rabbigs met a colourful cat, who was wearing a tall blue hat,
They started to greet with a slice of meat,
And they went to the woods and played Puddy-hud
For hours on end, till they went round the bend,
Is the land where the Rabbigs live.

Far and away, far and away
Is the land where the Rabbigs live,
Their heads are pink and their hands are red
And they never get out of their bed, bed, bed,
They never get out of their bed.

Abigail Wallis & Natasha Riches (10)
Roberttown J&I CE (C) School

Horses

There was a horse called Willow
Who lived in a big stable.
She could be very naughty
Because she eats cakes from the table.

Willow sometimes runs away,
She was once found at the station.
Her owner had to bring her back
To live on the sugar plantation.

Willow sometimes pulls the carriage
But only when she's attached with a cable.
When she trots along the road
She listens to a fable.

Willow has a fancy tail,
She is up for a nomination.
Let's hope she wins an award
At the Jubilee presentation.

Kerry Murphy (10)
Roberttown J&I CE (C) School

The Colours Poem

What is green? The grass is green,
Smelling fresh and clean.
What is black? Black is a witch's cat
Creeping up to a big fat rat.
What is white? Snow is white
Melting in the sunlight.
What is blue? The sea is blue,
Salty and very cold too!
What is brown? Chocolate is brown,
As lovely as a golden crown.
What is orange? Why I do not know so . . .
My poem will have to stop here!

Georgia Trevitt
Roberttown J&I CE (C) School

Midsummer's Eve

On a midsummer's eve
The forest sways in the breeze.

On a midsummer's eve
The water ripples
And the forest sways in the breeze.

On a midsummer's eve
The mountains climb,
The water ripples
And the forest sways in the breeze.

On a midsummer's eve
The animals call,
The mountains climb,
The water ripples
And the forest sways in the breeze.

On a midsummer's eve
The reeds whistle,
The animals call,
The mountains climb,
The water ripples
And the forest sways in the breeze.

On a midsummer's eve
The boats bob up and down,
The reeds whistle,
The animals call,
The mountains climb,
The water ripples
And the forest sways in the breeze.

On a midsummer's eve
You write a poem,
What would you write about?

Alasdair Hurst (10)
Roberttown J&I CE (C) School

How Doth The Furry Monkey . . .

How doth the furry monkey
Improve his swinging from tree to tree
And comb his perfect fur
And goes to collect the bananas up for his tea?

How carefully he opens his bananas,
How neatly he swings
And when he has finished swinging from tree to tree
He then puts on his stripy pyjamas
And goes to bed and sees what the night brings.

Ella Pearson-Glover (8)
Roberttown J&I CE (C) School

Special Time

Christmas time
Brings lots of joy, children
Opening their new toys sitting in front
Of the fire glow, snug inside
All out of the
Snow. Spring is here,
Once again see the flowers
Make my day, a lot are out in early
May, picking flowers making my day.

Megan Cunliffe (10)
Roberttown J&I CE (C) School

A Journey Through My Senses

I would like to see the fresh colourful air dancing on the wind,
I would like to hear the sparkling colours of the rainbow and stars,
I would like to smell the moon when it is dark,
I would wish to touch the outside of the Earth,
I would like to taste the planet Mars.

Will Banyard (7)
Roberttown J&I CE (C) School

A Poor Old Gardener

A poor old gardener said, 'Ah me!
My days are almost done,
I've got rheumatics in my knee
And now it's hard to run.
I've got measles on my foot
And chilblains on my nose,
And bless me if I haven't got
Pneumonia in my toes!

All my hair has fallen out
And my teeth have fallen in.
I really am getting rather stout,
Although I'm much too thin.
My nose is deaf and my ears are dumb,
My tongue is tied in knots
And now my barrow and my spade
Have all come out in spots.
In all my life I have only won,
A pumpkin in a pot.'

Christopher Thomas (11)
Roberttown J&I CE (C) School

Journey Through My Senses

I would like to see the wind dancing towards me,
I would like to hear a shape talking to me,
I would like to touch the stars,
I would like to smell the moon,
I would like to stay happy forever and ever,
I would like to taste the rainbow so I know what it tasted like.

Stevie Chanteleau (8)
Roberttown J&I CE (C) School

A Dream Is Like Your Friend!

A dream is like your friend,

A dream is a flower that always grows,
A friend is love that never dies.

A dream is like your friend.

A dream is a light, a candlelight lasting forever,
A friend is the bulb of a big, gorgeous, everlasting rose.

A dream is like your friend.

A dream is imagination, piled in your mind,
A friend is a girl like Amy who makes my day.

A dream is a true friend!

Hannah Pickering (9)
Roberttown J&I CE (C) School

Roses Are Red

Roses are red,
Vikings are blue.
The Saxons are happy
Since Alfred beat you!

Megan Preston (8)
Roberttown J&I CE (C) School

War

War is a place where people fight,
Some people die and it is ever so sad.
Married men who die leave their wives without a husband,
War should be stopped.

Joel Robinson (7)
Roberttown J&I CE (C) School

On My Way To School

On my way to school I saw a dragon.
On my way to school I saw a green dragon.
On my way to school I saw a gentle, kind, green dragon.
On my way to school I saw a spotted, gentle, kind, green dragon.
On my way to school I saw a big, spotted, gentle, kind, green dragon.

On my way to school I saw a snake.
On my way to school I saw a pink snake.
On my way to school I saw a mean, pink snake.
On my way to school I saw an ugly, mean, pink snake.
On my way to school I saw a vicious, ugly, mean, pink snake.

On my way to school I saw an elephant.
On my way to school I saw a grey elephant.
On my way to school I saw a shiny, grey elephant.
On my way to school I saw a hungry, shiny, grey elephant.
On my way to school I saw a hard, hungry, shiny, grey elephant.

Liam Gallagher (8)
Roberttown J&I CE (C) School

Tiger! Tiger!

Tiger, tiger you scare me,
You are striped with black and orange fur,
You have black and white eyes.
Creeping behind me
You made me jump high in the middle of the moonlight
And you gave me a great big fright.
Your body is long,
Your tail is short,
You like to play a sport.

Danielle Cornforth (7)
Roberttown J&I CE (C) School

On The Track

On the track
Ready to go
The engine roars up
And away they go

Racing around rough and tough
Hitting hard as they move

Faster and faster around the track
The chequered flag drops
For the race to be stopped

In the pits
The wheels come off
The engine refuelled
For the next race to come.

Jack David Collins (10)
Roberttown J&I CE (C) School

The Best Dragon

The best dragon is very fierce,
It waits around
In the land of dragons,
Bosses other dragons around
And sometimes takes baby dragons for a ride,
Blowing higher,
Is very scary
In the land of dragons.
Here comes a dragon
Look out quick
And they go
With a flick!

Jamie Crowther (7)
Roberttown J&I CE (C) School

Snow

Falling, falling everywhere,
Then sticking to the ground,
Look out of the window,
Then turning all around,
Duvet covers wrapped around tight,
Nice and warm at midnight,
Morning comes brilliant white,
Trees and roof tops
Sparkling bright.

Bethany Robinson (9)
Roberttown J&I CE (C) School

What Is?

What is red? A motorbike is red,
That I can just imagine in my head.
What is pink? A panther is pink,
And when I look at it it makes me blink.
What is green? A car is green,
That is gleamy clean.
What is blue? Glue is blue,
But blue sure gives me the flu.

Oliver Hedges-Hemingway (8)
Roberttown J&I CE (C) School

A Journey Through My Senses

I would like to see the wind dancing on the sand,
I would like to hear the toast burning on the sun,
I would like to touch the fiery sun and burn the other planets,
I would like to smell the shining colours of the rainbow,
I would like to taste the shining stars.

Helen Edmond (8)
Roberttown J&I CE (C) School

As I Was Going To Leeds

As I was going to Leeds
I saw a man planting seeds,
Each seed had six pounds,
Each pound had seven hounds.

Each hound had eight jewels,
Each jewel had ten fools,
Seeds, pounds, hounds, jewels, fools,
How many were going to Leeds?

Jack Baldwin (9)
Roberttown J&I CE (C) School

Swimming With Whales

I went to my swimming class
And guess what I found?
I saw a gigantic killer whale
It was swimming round and round.
If you need some help
It will come up and save you
And its name was Silver Killer
He leapt in the air and flew . . .

Jonathan Pickering (7)
Roberttown J&I CE (C) School

A Journey Through My Senses

I would like to see the stretched, smooth fresh air waking up me
I would like to hear a slimy crackly snake talk to me
I would like to touch the colourfully sparkly rainbow
I would like to smell the man eating cheese
I would like to taste the hot blazing sun.

Megan Enevoldson (8)
Roberttown J&I CE (C) School

School

Science, maths, English, history,
These are my favourite subjects in school.
Science is fun,
English is done,
Now maths 1, 2, 3, 4,
Finally history, is there any more?

Art, design, reading, geography
These are my favourite subjects in school.
Geography is cool,
Reading a rhyme,
Is done all the time,
Design a book,
Art is coming up,
So have a look.
I love school,
So why don't you?

Sara-Jayne Pollard (10)
Roberttown J&I CE (C) School

I Would Like Poem

I would like to see
chocolates melting in the tin

I would like to hear the shining
stars twinkle on the world

I would like to smell the
birds tweeting in the fresh air

I would like to touch the cold
magic coming to me

I would like to taste the
scrumptious taste of the dark night.

Jordan Brunt (8)
Roberttown J&I CE (C) School

The End

Cold is foot and heart and bone
And cold is sleep under stone
When grass is green on the other side
And you have failed, although you tried

The end of us, the end of us all
Answering to evil's call
No more to sleep on stony bed,
When sun is faded, and moon is dead.

Simon J Gray (10)
Roberttown J&I CE (C) School

The Sun

I like it when the sun comes out to play on a very shiny day,
and the horses are out to run having so much fun,
and I have lots of fun, and I can play in the sun,
and when I have been so busy
and I go to bed with my belly well fed,
and say, 'Goodnight
Sleep tight . . . '

Eva Hague (7)
Roberttown J&I CE (C) School

Sunflakes

If sun fell like snowflakes we could build a sunman
and have a sunball fight.
We could go sleighing in the middle of July
We could watch sunflakes dithering in the sky
To let them fall upon my hand.

I wonder how they feel?

Laura Baldwin (11)
Roberttown J&I CE (C) School

Crying Girl

A girl in the cloakroom
won't go out to play
waiting for the bullies to go away
not a sound except for weeping
staying till tomorrow evening
a bully passes
as food changes to ashes
a friend comes, a smile on her face
a party invitation in her hand
the bullies stop and stare
she doesn't feel lonely anymore.

Kirsty Crowther (9)
Roberttown J&I CE (C) School

Moonlight

Moonlight is a thing that never goes away.
Moonlight is a thing that everybody loves.
Moonlight is a thing that no one will destroy.
Moonlight is the thing that everybody enjoys.

Matthew Brook (10)
Roberttown J&I CE (C) School

My Mum

My mum is special
My mum is kind
My mum is busy
And we can read her mind.

Billie Terry (8)
Roberttown J&I CE (C) School

Kangaroo

Into the jungle cave came a kangaroo
Into the jungle cave came a bouncing kangaroo
Into the jungle cave came a bouncing, giant kangaroo
Into the jungle cave came a bouncing, giant, brown kangaroo
Into the jungle cave came a bouncing, giant, brown, red, spotty
    kangaroo
Into the jungle cave came a bouncing, giant, brown, red, spotty,
    dancing kangaroo
Into the jungle cave came a bouncing, giant, brown, red, spotty,
    dancing, leaping kangaroo
Into the jungle cave came a bouncing, giant, brown, red, spotty,
    dancing, leaping, hopping kangaroo
Into the jungle cave came a bouncing, giant, brown, red, spotty,
    dancing, leaping, hopping, joyful kangaroo
Into the jungle cave came a bouncing, giant, brown, red, spotty,
    dancing, leaping, hopping, joyful, giddy kangaroo.

Amy Blackburn (8)
Roberttown J&I CE (C) School

Darkness

When the golden sun sets
The darkness falls
You can hear the wolf call.

The glistening stars in the sky
The darkness is here
The wolf is near.

The moon starts to set
And the sun is met
Again.

Laylaa Whittaker (9)
Roberttown J&I CE (C) School

What Is . . . ?

What is pink? Pink is a flower
like a very tall tower.

What is red? Red is my bed
where I rest my head.

What is blue? Blue is the sky
where birds fly by.

What is green? Green is grass
like shiny brass.

What is yellow? Yellow is the sun
like the icing of a bun.

What is purple? Purple is my book
where I sit and look.

What is orange? Why, an orange
is just an orange.

Sonnie Terry (9)
Roberttown J&I CE (C) School

A Journey Through My Senses

I would like to touch the air.
I would like to hear the Earth spinning around.
I would like to see the clouds of colours.
I would like to smell the sun having dinner.
I would love to have sight so that
I could see the greatest place above Earth.
I would like to taste the sun.
I would like to feel happy all the time.

Matthew Haigh (7)
Roberttown J&I CE (C) School

I Would . . .

I would love to see
the rainbow dancing on the sea.

I would like to smell
the colours of the rainbow.

I would like to hear
the fish cuddling up to the moon.

I would like to touch the stars.

I would like to taste the moon.

Jarda Clayton (7)
Roberttown J&I CE (C) School

The Mountains

The mountains are bare,
The mountains are cold,
The mountains are covered with snow.
The mountains are cloudy,
The mountains are rocky,
The mountains are a beautiful sight.
Skiers ski down them,
Birds fly above them,
I'd love to visit the mountains.

Katie Miller (11)
Roberttown J&I CE (C) School

Untitled

How doth the little elephant
Improve his laughing skills?
And when he puts on his underpants
He takes his swimming pills.

Lauren Kitson (8)
Roberttown J&I CE (C) School

I Met A . . .

I met a fish
Who made a wish

I met a mouse
Who had a house

I met a frog
Who sat on a log

I met a goat
Who had a sore throat

I met a bee
As big as a tree

I met a cat
Who was blind as a bat

I met a hen
Who was in a den

I met a rabbit
Who had a bad habit

I met an owl
With a great big scowl

I met a horse
It was big of course

I met a whale
That was for sale

I met a shark
That could sing like a lark

I met a chimp
Who was a wimp

I met a pig
Who had a wig

I met a bear
Who had no hair

I met a tiger
Who had a tickle inside her

I met a cow
But I don't know how

I met a sheep
Oh! I was asleep.

Robyn Michaela Smith (10)
Roberttown J&I CE (C) School

Annapura

Climbing, getting higher and higher,
With each step.
Oxygen mask on,
Pressing against my face.

Colder, getting higher and higher,
Can't feel my feet anymore.
Even with six layers on,
The cold still gets in.

Whiter, getting higher and higher,
Snow on the top.
Getting harder to breathe,
A few more steps.

At last, it was all worth it,
Stopping to catch breath.
The view amazing,
Never seen anything like it.

On top of the world!

Kerry Busby (11)
Roberttown J&I CE (C) School

Samurai

With his great broad armour
Armed with his sword
He slays all his foes, the Samurai lord

With his swift and his skills
He brings down a dragon
He hides and escapes in an old, battered wagon

He chews through his food
With his straight, well-cleaned teeth,
He takes out his dagger and
Puts them to sleep.

Who is he?
He's a Samurai!

Tom Allatt (11)
Roberttown J&I CE (C) School

My Mum

My mum is lovely
My mum is kind
She works as hard as you'll ever find
I don't mind

My mum's age is thirty-nine
She truly is a wife
Her favourite animal is a
Black and white fluffy dog
Covered in snow from the fog
It isn't that hard to help
Just think what you do and shout
'Yelp!'

Rachel Glaves (6)
Roberttown J&I CE (C) School

Into The Garden Strode A Horse

Into the garden strode a horse
Into the garden strode a nice horse
Into the garden strode a nice, lovely horse
Into the garden strode a nice, lovely, kind horse
Into the garden strode a nice, lovely, kind, gentle horse
Into the garden strode a nice, lovely, kind, gentle, helpful horse
Into the garden strode a nice, lovely, kind, gentle, helpful, curious
                                                                                          horse.

Isabel Oldroyd (7)
Roberttown J&I CE (C) School

George Fought A Dragon

George fought a dragon
George fought a one-eyed dragon
George fought a stinky, one-eyed dragon
George fought a fat, stinky, one-eyed dragon
George fought a foul, fat, stinky, one-eyed dragon
George fought an ugly, foul, fat, stinky, one-eyed dragon.

George Bartle (7)
Roberttown J&I CE (C) School

Penguin

I came across a penguin on the way to school
His fur was very fluffy and his beak was very hard
I hid him in my PE kit so that the teacher would not see
He stayed there very quietly until he was frightened by a bee.

Joseph Lancaster (8)
Roberttown J&I CE (C) School

Nonsense Poem

Sophie in America
Lives in Jamaica
She has three children
Because she's married to a baker.
Ten kids in a bedroom,
Were playing in a bathroom,
Riding a broom.
People in Brazil,
Daily walk up a hill,
As the world thinks that they are brill.
Lily from Turkey,
Always looks perky,
After a boat journey.
People from Ireland,
Dream of pie-land,
But end up digging sand.
Alan from Mexico,
Always hosts a talent show,
He really likes it when they sing and dance
If they come from France.

Rachel Brook (10)
St Ignatius Catholic Primary School, Ossett

Things I Don't Like

Slimy snails sliding,
Wiggly worms wriggling,
Great gazelles gliding,
Giant geese or gander.

Sly sharks swimming,
Fierce falcons fighting,
Silly swallows singing,
Horrible hyenas hysterically laughing.

Catherine Thompson (11)
St Ignatius Catholic Primary School, Ossett

Sunshine

Sun, sun, sizzling sun,
Shining on my hot cross bun,
Shimmering on my teddy bear,
Also on my sleek brown hair.

I see a colourful rainbow,
Lurking in the dark shadow,
I wonder if it's going to rain,
I look outside once again.

The clouds are black,
The storm is back,
I see the drizzling rain,
Running down the windowpane.

What happened to the sizzling sun
Shining on my hot cross bun?

Siobhan Ann Crossland (11)
St Ignatius Catholic Primary School, Ossett

Around The World And Back!

From England to Spain, it starts to rain!
From Spain to France, I've lost my pants!
From France to Greece, I've bought a fleece!
From Greece to Chile, the pilot's name's Billy!
From Chile to Japan, I've got a tan!
From Japan to Hong Kong, it's all wrong!
From Hong Kong to Menorca, the place is a corker!
From Menorca to the North Pole, I'm down a hole!
From the North Pole to Arabia, they'll want to slave ya!
From Arabia to England - there's my house, I'm home!

Leo Hughes (11)
St Ignatius Catholic Primary School, Ossett

Conversational Poem

Carra said, 'If I were a bell I'd like ringing.'
Edward said, 'If I were a bird I'd like singing.'
Carra said, 'If I were an ant I'd like creeping.'
Edward said, 'If I were a lion I'd like sleeping.'
Carra said, 'If I were a shark I'd like biting.'
Edward said, 'If I were a pirate I'd like fighting.'
Carra said, 'If I were a mouse I'd like snatching.'
Edward said, 'If I were a cat I'd like scratching.'
Carra said, 'If I were a pig I'd like rolling.'
Edward said, 'If I were good at it I'd like bowling.'
Carra said, 'If I were a snake I'd like sliding.'
Edward said, 'If I were a hedgehog I'd like hiding.'
Carra said, 'If I were a horse I'd like eating hay.'
Edward said, 'If I were a teacher I'd probably have
                              something else to say.'

Caitlin Davies (10)
St Ignatius Catholic Primary School, Ossett

Books

Books, books and more books,
Fiction, picture and info.
Study all night and
Study all day.
Books, books and books.

Books, books and more books.
What shall we do today?
Read all day and read all night
Books, books and books!

Nicola Perkins & Joseph Finnigan (11)
St Ignatius Catholic Primary School, Ossett

School, School, School

Dictionary on the shelf,
Pencil in hand,
Why do all this work,
Can't we make a band?

School, school, school

Literacy and numeracy,
Assemblies in the hall,
Why do all this work?
We'd rather play football.

School, school, school

Sums are a bore,
Adding up all day,
Why do all this work,
When we'd rather play?

School, school, school

Playing without learning,
This may seem so grand,
But working hard in school,
Gives you the upper hand.

School, school, school.

Matthew Lowrey (10)
St Ignatius Catholic Primary School, Ossett

The Wicked Wallaby

I am the wicked wallaby.
I don't eat shrubs, grass or herbs,
I chomp and chew beefburgers and chips.
I don't jump and hop around,
I go ice skating and surfing.
I am not your average coloured wallaby.
I am purple!
I am the wicked wallaby!

Phoebe Williams (8)
St Mary's CE School, Boston Spa

The Meeting

A bustling square . . .
People pushing, shoving, milling about.
Suddenly, a shadow,
A fervent handclasp,
A warm handshake.
'Hello, Peter.'
I grow dizzy, shake my head,
Where have I heard that voice before?
An unstruck bell struck, tuned, then struck again.
An age old sword, gathering dust,
Shaken, then polished until it shines once again.
The memory floods back.
'Hello, Vincente,' I say
And there we are,
Two old school friends
In the middle of a busy square,
Shaking hands
And laughing.

James Hibbert (10)
St Mary's CE School, Boston Spa

If You Want To See A Tiger

If you want to see a tiger
you must down to the old African jungle.

When you go down to the old African jungle,
you must shout,
'Growly tiger,
Growly tiger,
Growly tigerrrrrr.'

But up he'll step,
don't stay around.
Run for your life!

Amy Uttley (8)
St Mary's CE School, Boston Spa

Season Fairies

The bulbs we bring at the first signs of spring
Bringing life and lambs to Earth; giving the world new birth
Bringing the flowers that used to wilt
Making them tall rather than tilt
In the early morn the birds do sing
Brighten the sun and everything.

There is the sun high in the sky
Brightening all passing by
Children play in the park until late when it gets dark
Parents relax by the pool, or on holiday where the breeze is cool
Ice lollies melting in the heat
The summer break is such a treat
In the flowers there are bees
On the beach there is clear blue sea.

The leaves fall down filling the town
Picking apples red and green
Careful not to miss those in-between
In and out the north wind blows rustling the grass as it grows
Farmers harvest up their crop
Water's colder in the loch
Leaves in colours red and gold
All the weather getting cold.

Icy winds, chilly snow making noses glow
Hats and scarves and woolly gloves
And warm hot chocolate in mugs
Go ice skating in the park
Go home early or it will be dark.

All of the changes the seasons bring
Remember us fairies and the song that we sing.

Cordelia Keston (9)
St Mary's CE School, Boston Spa

Fly Little Bird

Fly little bird,
Fly if you can.
Or you could end up
In a pan.

Fly, fly,
quick as you can,
Some people want you
In a pan.

You are tender,
But you are small.
Fly little bird,
Fly for your sake,
Or you will end up
In a pan.

Move fast little bird,
They have big bows and arrows
And they will shoot you
For you are fat,
And they will stop at nothing
To catch you and eat you.

This is my last call little bird,
Come to me now.
Thank you, thank you,
Safe with me again.

Alexander Hibbert (7)
St Mary's CE School, Boston Spa

My Friends

At the end of the school day,
I go out to play,
With the friends that I meet
At the end of the street.
My friend Sam has a body that is very bendy,
He wears nice clothes and is very trendy.
My friend Harry has a cool bike with suspension,
And three girlfriends we don't like to mention.
Also, Harry is very tall,
Next to him, my friend Alex is very small.
Ellie's a girl but quite fun,
Because every time she brings a gun.
Lastly there is me, I like playing PlayStation,
On my own TV.
I am also very cool,
Because I beat adults at playing pool.
I hope you like my little rhyme,
And this is how we spend our time.

Bradley Kitching (8)
St Mary's CE School, Boston Spa

Taste

I love the taste of . . .
Shiny, crunchy apples,
Hot, spicy chicken tikka masala,
Greasy, salty bacon straight from the pan,
Tomatoey, meaty spaghetti Bolognese,
Freezing, tooth-aching ice cream,
Long, lovely pepperoni sticks,
Hot chocolate still warm, with a thick layer of chocolate on top,
Candyfloss like a spider's web in a ball.
Delicious!

Polly Whitelam (9)
St Mary's CE School, Boston Spa

Once Upon A Time

Once upon a time,
Stars all brightly shine.
Fairies dancing,
Pixies prancing,
Once upon a time.

Tales of missing shoes
And princes finding
Girls so loving,
Once upon a time.

Witches brewing spells,
Princesses sleeping,
By kisses waking,
Once upon a time.

Christmas fairy tales
Of Santa flying,
And reindeer gliding,
Once upon a time.

Princesses and fairies,
Poor boys and rich kings,
Giants ever so scary,
Once upon a time.
But this is a poem,
So it has to be
Once upon a *rhyme!*

Eve McQuillan (10)
St Mary's CE School, Boston Spa

Before The Big Day

Sunny breeze
Warms me.
Crazy fans
Cheer me.
Spring water
Refreshes me.
Floodlights
Light my way
To the goal.
As the coach
Leads the premier team
To the blue ribbon,
So may I
Escape my injuries
In this final game.
Happy supporters
Encourage us,
Football fans
Boost us,
TV cameras
Capture me,
Lead me to
My victory.

James Coates (8)
St Mary's CE School, Boston Spa

Snow

I love it when the silky snow is drifting down
And falls on your cold feet,
When the bare trees shiver in the winter's snow,
All the birds ruffle up their warm feathers.
We all wrap up warmly, put on our coats,
Scarves and gloves.
Most insects die in the winter and some birds leave us.
I love snow.

Jessica Heaton (7)
St Mary's CE School, Boston Spa

Whale Watching

Today I woke bright and early
between the hours of four and five,
to see great big sperm whales
do a spout and deep, deep dive!

I flew to the side of the boat,
saw pilot whales and dolphins.
The captain used his hydrophone
to hear the sperm whale clicking.

And then I saw it,
through the wave,
a spouting in the distance
in the Bay of Kaikoura.

I saw a sperm whale,
I saw a pilot whale,
And then I saw a bottlenose dolphin.

Natalie Heaton (10)
St Mary's CE School, Boston Spa

-12°C

Reindeer hooves go clip-clop, clip-clop
Huskies bark as they pull the sleigh
Where am I?

Santa Claus sits with children all around him
And a sack filled with toys to give away.
Where am I?

I get a snowmobile with no hassle
And skid along the snow 'til I find an ice castle.
Where am I?

I am in *Lapland*.

Naomi Barrow (9)
St Mary's CE School, Boston Spa

Colours

Yellow daffodils make me happy
Pink wrapping paper makes my birthday
Blue napkins make me clean
Red hats, gloves and scarves make me warm
Black darkness makes me scared
Silver stars make me happy and cheerful
Yellow sun makes me cosy
Grey wintry clouds make me sad
Pink Barbie dolls make me happy, happy, happy!

Roxanne Frost (7)
St Mary's CE School, Boston Spa

The Sun

The sun beams,
leans on the garden wall
like an egg laid on hay.
Shiny sun.

The sun shines,
limes squeezed in glasses
like yellow peaches on a fruit bowl.
Light.

Emma Whitaker (8)
St Mary's CE School, Boston Spa

The Roller Coaster

Whizzing in and out on wobbly tracks,
Loop-the-loops making me jump in the capsule,
Flyovers making me shout with fear,
Going upside down, hurting me on the safety belt,
Roller coasters are cool!

Jonathan Barrow (8)
St Mary's CE School, Boston Spa

Fish

Fish, fish, multicoloured fish
Swimming in the deep, deep ocean.
Fish, fish, multicoloured fish
In every shape and size.

Fish, fish, multicoloured fish
From angler fish to minnow.
Fish, fish, multicoloured fish
Swimming in the deep, deep ocean.

Eleri Dorsett-Paynton (7)
St Mary's CE School, Boston Spa

Elvis Presley

Chunky cheek bones,
Jet-black hair,
Winning smile,
Bushy eyebrows,
Twinkling hazel eyes,
Blue suede shoes,
The king of rock and roll.
Elvis Presley.

Grace Barrett (9)
St Mary's CE School, Boston Spa

Homework

H orrible headaches
O dd additions
M ore work
E very night!
W asting my playtime
O vercasting my fun
R acing through it
K eeping in mind I'm almost done!

Jamie Taylor (8)
St Mary's CE School, Boston Spa

Dear Mum

Summer camp is making me really glum
The most I've had to eat is a tiny little crumb
But enough complaining, you know I'm feigning
Just to make you take me home.
Here's some of the things I've done:

I've been scuba-diving, go-kart drivin'
Sunbathin' in the sun.
I've been backwoods cookin', big fish hookin'
And you'll never guess how far I've had to run.
But that's not really anything to write home about,
Take me home!

I've been white water raftin', totem pole craftin',
And I've learnt some really funny puns!
I've slept in a log cabin, I've also been campin'
And I've cooked some really tasty buns.
But that's not really anything to write home about,
Take me home!

OK, so that's what I've done, it's really fun
And my clothes need a wash; they're starting to reek,
But please can I stay for another week?

John,
Your son.

Liam Livesley (9)
St Mary's CE School, Boston Spa

The Water Giant

The Water Giant marching down
To terrorise the tiny town
Upon his head a giant crown
Made of thistle berries.

Around the town a wall of slat
The Water Giant sees to that
By smashing it with his giant hat
Made of thistle berries.

The townspeople run and scream
Around the town, around the stream
But they can't escape the giant's dream
Made of thistle berries.

Philip Rodger (11)
St Mary's CE School, Boston Spa

The Moon

A full moon is like a yellow apple with no stalk,
Hanging from an invisible tree.
Like a shiny dinner plate,
Washed in a golden ball.

A crescent moon is like a banana flying down into the sea,
Whizzing round and round.
Like a toucan's beak,
Singing with its tongue out.

Joshua Kidd (8)
St Mary's CE School, Boston Spa

My Three Cats

I have a cat called Sid
Who sits on the bin lid.
When I walk past he purrs
At me and jumps on my back.

I have a cat called George
Who's shy all the time.
He likes to lay all day,
But sometimes likes to play.

I have a cat called Bobby
Who likes to play,
He chases his tail round and round
And falls on the ground.

Kate Towns (8)
St Mary's CE School, Boston Spa

Flower Fairies

They are in all kinds of places,
They come out in any season,
They look after flowers and trees,
The blossom and the berries,
They watch the flowers growing,
The children having fun,
They like the warming sunshine,
The bees and butterflies.
They are very elegant
With their beautiful wings
And tiny, careful hands.
There's only one thing they can be:
Flower fairies!

Léonie Ricard (7)
St Mary's CE School, Boston Spa

Football Time

Saturday mornings, get up early,
Football time.
Cold and blustery, wet and windy,
Football time.
Arriving late, run round pitch,
Football time.
Kicking around, defending and attacking,
Football time.
I get up to the halfway point,
Football time.
Try to shoot, I hear my teammates calling,
Football time.
Aim, kick and I score!
Football time.
I love football.

Naomi Allan (11)
St Mary's CE School, Boston Spa

Autumn Days

As the autumn gradually grows the wind prunes the trees
The autumn colours flow as the migrating birds flee
The tossing and turning leaves flutter overhead
The scenery is blending scarlet and mustard changing every petal
The rusted leaves dance around
Swooping as autumn breathes
The howling echoes bounce off the colourful trees
Fearing to go in the woods
As the rustling leaves gently rust, they fall to the ground
The needle conker shells lay in a path waiting to be discovered
All the children returning to their treasured tree, none left to be found.
Autumn, the most wonderful season of them all.

Matthew Bulley (9)
St Mary's CE School, Boston Spa

What's My Pet?

I have a pet
His name is Titch,
He's got lots of fur,
He likes to itch.
Can you guess what he is?

He is quite friendly
And playful too,
He'll run about the house
And start licking you.
Can you guess what he is?

My friends came around,
He started jumping about,
He licked their faces,
You'd better watch out!
Can you guess what he is?

Bethany Horner (10)
Sacred Heart RC Primary School

The A-Z Of Food, Food, Food

Apples, bananas, food is the best,
Cherries, doughnuts, food is better than the rest,
Eggs, fries, food is to be,
Gherkins, hamburgers, food is your tea,
Ice cream, jelly, food must go on,
KitKats, lemons, food is number one,
Munchies, nuts, food is great,
Oranges, peaches, food you can't hate,
Quavers, rice, food you can buy,
Sausages, turnips, without food you would die,
Unsweetened biscuits, vanilla slices, some foods are sweet,
Weetabix, Oxo, some foods are a treat,
Yoghurt, a zesty fruit, you're always in the mood,
That's why I love food, food, food.

Lili Cordingley (9)
Sacred Heart RC Primary School

Rainbow

Red, yellow, pink and green
These are the colours I have seen
Red are the roses that grow so sweet,
Yellow is the corn that gives us wheat,
Pink are the lilies that are so small,
Green is the grass that grows very tall.

Orange, purple and blue
These are the colours I have dreamt of too.
Orange is the sunshine that glows in the sky,
Purple is the lavender that is so shy,
Blue is the river that flows so high.

Brown, black, grey and white,
These are the colours that have no light.
Brown are the beetles that scurry around,
Black is the mud that is underground,
Grey are the cloudy clouds that float across the sky,
White are the stars that fly, fly, fly,
But why did the rainbow make so much,
Why, why, why?

Amie Scott (10)
Sacred Heart RC Primary School

Beautiful School

School, school, beautiful school,
It is extremely cool,
They even have a swimming pool
They like art
But don't like maths
And a pet dog called Cool.
They have a monkey called Max,
He sings all day and doesn't get away.

Samantha Rudge (9)
Sacred Heart RC Primary School

Seasons

Spring is the beginning,
When daffodils grow,
Birds return from foreign lands
And the land begins to glow.

Summer is the time when children play,
Laughter floating in the air,
Trees and fields all green and bright,
Water splashing everywhere.

Autumn leaves floating down,
Red, yellow, golden-brown.
Wind begins to howl and blow,
Animals wrap up safe and warm.

Winter snow shining crisp and bright,
Icicles dancing to the moonlight,
All the flowers go to sleep,
Daylight shortens, turns to night.

Micheala Mason (10)
Sacred Heart RC Primary School

I Wish

I wish I was a bird,
I'd fly away.
I wish I had a pet,
To play with every day.

I wish I had magic powers,
To spook people out.
I wish I was really good,
So my mum would never shout.

I wish I had a massive swimming pool,
I'd go swimming every day.
I wish my mum paid for everything,
I'd never have to pay.

Jake Brown (9)
Sacred Heart RC Primary School

My Hobbies

I like playing football,
I play for Crossley's U10s.
My friends and I are so good,
Maybe this year we will win the cup.
I am the goalie,
I try to keep a clean sheet.
My coach is called Mick,
We have to train very hard,
I get muddy and wet,
But it is all worth it in the end.

I like swimming,
I swim for Halifax Swimming Club.
My friends and I are so good,
Maybe this year we will win the championship.
My favourite stroke is butterfly,
I race against time.
My trainer is called Gill.
We have to train very hard,
I get very tired,
But it is all worth it in the end.

Joshua Berry (9)
Sacred Heart RC Primary School

Chocolate

C rispy and crunchy
H ot and gooey
O range and mint
C aramel delight
O nce you've tried, you won't stop
L ovely and luscious
A ll the time
T ry it now
E veryone has.

Lucy Mitchell (9)
Sacred Heart RC Primary School

I Went On Holiday To Malham

I went on holiday to Malham,
I walked across the cove,
It was so cold and so windy,
I almost fell off.

The next day I went fishing,
The only thing I caught was a couple of fish.
I cooked them for tea,
They were ever so tasty.

The wind was so strong
It blew over my tent,
In my pyjamas I rolled over
And hurt my neck again.

At last it was breakfast time,
Bacon, eggs, sausage and beans,
Just for me.
How am I supposed to walk miles and miles today?

I started walking, I fell halfway,
I can't wait to get a good tea.
I am getting out of here,
Hip, hip, hooray.

When I got there I went to bed,
I had a dream of Malham in my holiday.

Joseph Milner (9)
Sacred Heart RC Primary School

What Am I?

I live in the ocean,
I live in the sea,
I wear suntan lotion,
So what can I be?

I am very small,
I hate sharks,
And I love going to water parks,
So what can I be?

I have big ears
And a long nose,
And very, very, very big toes,
So what can I be?

I am a bird
But I cannot fly,
I live in the Arctic,
So what am I?

Joe Fletcher (9)
Sacred Heart RC Primary School

My Life

Once I went fishing, I didn't catch much.
I had lots of fun, I ate a big bun.
But the catch of the day was in some pain,
But at the end of the day I was in pain.
Joe I caught, so he hit me with a cane.

On the next day I went for a walk,
It wasn't much fun, there was nowhere to talk.
A bit further on I fell over,
Lauren laughed, so I knocked her over.

Alexander Wilson (9)
Sacred Heart RC Primary School

My Day Out

On the beach in the sand,
By the sea, crab on your knee,
I caught a fish,
Well, Dad did it for me.

Picnic time, yummy!
What's for lunch? Tuna sandwiches, scrummy.
Now it's time for Seaworld,
There's a whale, there's a shark.
Argh! It's going to eat me!

Going home,
But I don't want to,
I want to stay.
But I will have lots of things
To tell my friends.
Hey you guys,
Wait for me.

Darrell Bingham (10)
Sacred Heart RC Primary School

My Family

My family is so cool, we have a pool,
We go in the pool to
Get so cool, we are so cool
Because we have
A big pool. Sometimes we
Are not so cool,
Because we sit in the room
And watch TV.

Peter Green (10)
Sacred Heart RC Primary School

My Family

My dad is so fat,
He lives in a flat.
He squashed a rat,
Oh he is so fat.

My brother is so skinny,
He lives in a Mini.
He is 58 metres tall,
Oh he is so skinny.

My mum is stretchy,
She touches infinity.
She eats lots of noodles,
Oh she is so stretchy.

My grandma is so wrinkly,
She is a bit stinky.
She needs a good iron,
Oh she is so wrinkly.

Robert Whitaker (10)
Sacred Heart RC Primary School

What Am I?

I'm a feather duster,
I'm a night flyer,
I'm a mice murderer,
I'm a tree nester,
I'm a moon gazer,
Day sleeper.

What am I?

Jemimah Crockford (9)
Sicklinghall CP School

The Shadows In The Street

A man is walking down a cobbled street,
All he can hear are his own two feet.

Looking back thinking someone's watching . . .

His heart starts pounding,
He picks up his pace.

He hears a spine-chilling noise,
His heart begins to race.

He breaks into a run wishing
He was in a different place.

But he suddenly sees his cosy house,
Can't wait till he's there - warm at last.

Before he knows it, he reaches his home
And sits by the fire - snug and alone.

Hetty Yoxall (11)
Sicklinghall CP School

What Am I?

A summer dweller,
A corn cutter,
A winter dunawer
A nine year survivor,
A hollow builder,
A corn eater,
A good gripper,
A tail rapper,
A snake hater,
A small runner.
What am I?

A: A harvest mouse.

James Woodhams (9)
Sicklinghall CP School

At The Beach

The sizzling sun shines all day
On the clear blue sea where we play.

We build sandcastles on the shore
And get covered in the sandy gore.

We munch sandy sandwiches
And lick lovely lollies.

When it's time to go home,
We have to pack up.

At night, a lonely man wanders the shore,
Sandcastles disappear one by one.

The lighthouse light slowly starts
Flashing round and round.

Waves crash together onto the shore
Soaking the man with water as
He sinks into the shadows of the sea.

Kali Popely (9)
Sicklinghall CP School

Fantasy World

Queuing for hours
With a scream in your ear,
Lurching stomachs
On roller coasters,
Ghostly faces
Lit by light,
Fireworks flying
In every direction.

Peaceful people
Laugh a lot,
Munching sounds
As they eat their KFC.
Tranquil rides twisting
This way and that,
Untroubled minds,
No worries at all.
As they leave their day of fantasy.

Naomi Probert (9)
Sicklinghall CP School

The Nobody

The cold, dark street
Where nobody walks,
Perishing with cold,
Its big feet numbing,
A snowy snowflake dropped
On its nose
I'm glad I'm not out there,
Because I'm inside my nice warm house,
Baking chestnuts in front of a fire,
Piping hot soup comes off the stove,
As the nobody comes by,
Offer it some soup,
Chuck it some chestnuts,
Then it won't be a nobody,
It will be a happy person,
That will mean one less sad one
In the world.

Lucie Almond (10)
Sicklinghall CP School

The Stormy Night

When I was in bed . . .

The windows were crashing,
The rain was slashing.

The thunder and lightning,
The twisting and turning.

The rain is falling,
The big puddles in the morning.

Now the sun is shining,
Have a picnic.

Sunbathing,
Lick our lovely lollipops.

Get the paddling pool out,
And *splash, splash, splash.*

Olivia Giddings (9)
Sicklinghall CP School

The Dolphin

A smooth swimmer
A wave surfer

A water whistler
A king acrobat

A youngster defender
A fish finder

A boat racer
A dinky diver

An enormous echoer
A herd maker

A squid swallower
A fast spinner.

Jamie Horwell (8)
Sicklinghall CP School

The Football Ground

The bustling of people,
The whistle of a man,
The kick of the ball,
The cheering of the crowd,
The scream of a goal,

And the sound of the final whistle.
All the crowd shouts and hisses.

The rustling of paper,
The rolling of a tin,

The wind is echoing,
The lawnmower growling,

The ground is hardening,
The roof is up,

The lights are out,
The door has locked.

The stadium is empty.

George Barton (9)
Sicklinghall CP School

Dale

There was a man from Spain,
Who was always a pain,
His name was Dale
And he drank a lot of ale,
But because he always lied,
He tumbled over and died.

Sophie Beeching-Smith (10)
Stanley St Peter's Primary School

Someone Annoying

There's someone really annoying,
She's always on cloud nine,
She constantly trips up,
But then she's always fine.

There's someone really annoying,
And when they try to laugh,
They get it wrong, it's like a snort,
Then she just looks daft.

There's someone really annoying,
They always get ignored,
It's simple why we do it,
She just makes us so bored.

There's someone really annoying,
They have hair like a bush,
She's always boasting how good she is,
Why won't she just shush?

There's someone really annoying,
She sticks her head in your face,
She's the smartest person I know,
They're such a headcase.

There's someone really annoying,
They show off all the time,
Why won't she be normal,
Or at least just mime?

There's someone really annoying,
They're just so *boring!*

Rebecca Doyle (10)
Stanley St Peter's Primary School

Christmas Is Coming

Christmas is coming
I can't wait
Presents in that chair
Not there.

Saint Nicholas is Santa
With his reindeer Rudolph
Where's the bear?
Tomorrow it is here.

Hurry up
Christmas is here soon,
I want a doll, some cars,
And some chocolate bars.

Come on Christmas!
I can't wait
Just hurry up
I want a pup.

Christmas is coming,
It is so near,
It is coming,
I can hear some drumming.

Christmas is here,
I just can't wait
Dad said,
I have to go to bed,
Christmas is coming.

Bethany Riding (10)
Stanley St Peter's Primary School

Valentine's Day

It's begun, Valentine's Day,
It's happening this Saturday,
This might sound stupid,
But I've been hit by Cupid,
I have found love,
Like a turtle dove,
And now 'I love you' is all I say.

You've left me alone,
And I've plunged like a stone,
But remember that arrow,
That's made me as sweet as a sparrow,
And I can't help but to follow
Until hopefully tomorrow,
Then maybe I won't follow you home.

Tomorrow has come,
But the arrow ain't done,
I'm unhappy, I can't settle,
I feel like I'm stung by a nettle,
I now really hate love,
I wish this feeling could shove,
So love's no longer fun.

I stick with what I've put,
As I might try love, but,
My love is not for you,
If you like me you can shoo,
'Cause you didn't when I was struck,
I had nothing but bad luck,
So now I've put down my foot.

Bethany Holroyd (11)
Stanley St Peter's Primary School

The Knight

The knight carried a sharp sword,
Which was gifted to him by his king and lord,
His shield was large with a silhouette of a dove,
He held it with his chainmail glove.

His steed was white and loyal,
His saddle was gold and fit for a royal,
He ran speedily and swift,
His blinkers were an earned gift.

The rider wore silver armour thick,
To protect him from even a horse's kick,
His helmet was gold to protect him from blows,
So he could survive attack from his foes.

He was sent to slay a banshee called Giffon,
If the banshee screams you must not listen,
The banshee screamed and the mount died,
Frozen dead on the floor it lied.

But the knight got his honour back,
He chopped off her head and put it in a sack,
For the knight now heir to the throne,
Had slain the banshee all on his own!

Robert Newiss (10)
Stanley St Peter's Primary School

I'll Be There

I'll be there for you (that's right),
I'll be waiting for you tonight,
I'll be there when you need me,
I'll be waiting for you by the sea.

I'll be at the café right on time,
I'll be up in the clouds on number nine,
I'll be, I'll be, I'll be, be, be,
I'll be there for you.

Katie Baigent (10)
Stanley St Peter's Primary School

About The Boy (Rap)

This special boy
Makes me feel
Great
But obviously I pretend
Hate
I think of him day
I think of him night
But if a girl was to
Take him
I'd put up a fight.

I'll be there when you
Need a mate but even
Better we could date
You know I wouldn't
Hesitate
Oh please, please, pick me
Up at eight.

Lauren Fawcett (11)
Stanley St Peter's Primary School

Together Forever

V alentine's Day has come,
A day for hugs and kisses,
L ove is most important,
E ven in cards, you might send it in,
N ever dying is my love,
T he friendship we share,
I n this life and forever on,
N ever dying is my love,
E ver love in the air.

D ays go by, whilst I wish this day stays,
A day of love and cherish, please . . .
Y ou stay, for you are my love.

Toni Mees (9)
Stanley St Peter's Primary School

A Monster In The Family

A monster in the family,
What are we gonna do?
It eats very messily,
The family's doomed!

A monster, a monster!
What are we gonna do?
He's not a very bright star,
We're better off hiding at Timbuktu.

But the strangest thing is,
When I shout my little brother's name,
It comes in a whiz.

Megan Croxall (11)
Stanley St Peter's Primary School

Hedgehog

Happy, helpful hedgehog,
Happy as can be,
Maybe he will come inside,
And see what's on for tea.
Look who's coming inside wet,
Sloshing mud everywhere,
Dry him off, dry him off,
So he's clean,
Coming on the big wide steps,
Following my doggy's muddy track,
On to his soft warm back,
Falling fast asleep.

Helen Dwyer (10)
Stanley St Peter's Primary School

My Hamster Milly

My hamster Milly is brown and white,
She is awake every minute at night,
She does my head in every day,
She likes to play and run away.

She lives in a little purple cage,
With her little house, she doesn't pay a wage,
She's sometimes scared when I go near,
And she sometimes trembles with fear.

Kirsty Palmer (10)
Stanley St Peter's Primary School

My Bedroom

I have a cream wall,
On my window ledge sits a signed football,
The signatures are Smith, Viduka and Harte,
On my wall is a picture of art,
Viduka is quite tall,
A marvel at heading the ball.

Kieran Wright (10)
Stanley St Peter's Primary School

There Was A Young Man

There was a young man from Spain,
Who helped the mayor to reign,
With the mayor's desire
He blew up with fire
And never was seen again.

Georgia Leigh Harris (10)
Stanley St Peter's Primary School

Ten Things Found In Harry Potter's Pocket

The strongest wand ever made,
A packet of magic powder,
A giant rabbit with floppy ears,
A brown broomstick,
An everlasting packet of sweets,
A tiny magic book,
An invisible cloak,
A giant cobra,
A pumpkin the size of an elephant's head,
An owl as white as snow,
All of this in Harry's pocket.

Sam Green (10)
Stanley St Peter's Primary School

In An Alien's Pocket

Eyeball from a hamster's cage,
Magic spaceship from Mars to Earth,
Spiders' webs from a bone to kill magic,
Glittering, dusty rocks from years and years ago,
Mucky nails from a baby girl
False teeth from his mouth to a mouse
Slavering wig to trick people too,
A fan to cool his sweaty loo
Fur from a mouldy rabbit just for you
Blood for his drink forever and ever.
Just like you!

Emma Coupland (10)
Stanley St Peter's Primary School

Ten Things Found In A Whale's Mouth

A boat full of people that
Were fishing in the sea,
A skeleton of a dead shark,
A whole house from Leeds,
A dark cloud from a rainy day,
A ringing telephone,
The whole sea with all the creatures,
A swimming pool for the humans to swim in,
Some toys to play with when he gets bored,
A bus shelter to wait for the bus,
And a bus to go to town in.

Abigail Couldwell (10)
Stanley St Peter's Primary School

Ten Things Found In A Horse's Pocket

A handful of oats to munch on,
Sixteen large carrots to eat,
A bucket of apple-flavoured water to drink,
A field of green grass to run around in,
A pink TV to watch Lizzie McGuire,
Ballet shoes to dance in,
A teacher to learn maths,
A book about ballet to read,
Reading glasses to wear so he can see what he is reading,
Red wine to drink with a table set for two.

Amy Shipley (10)
Stanley St Peter's Primary School

I Love My Dog

My dog is so much fun,
Her nose is like a shining sun,
She loves to play all day!
My dog is so cute,
Because she wears a fluffy suit,
My dog has black, shiny eyes,
Like little round cherry pies,
She loves to play all day,
I love my dog!

Hannah Brown (10)
Stanley St Peter's Primary School

Now In The Very Big House

Now the rain beat down on the very big house,
Now in the very big house lived a very small mouse,
Now the very small mouse had a problem, did he,
As in the very big house, a black cat roamed free,
Now the mouse set off for his lunch one day,
But the cat was stubborn and wanted to play,
Now the mouse he knew he'd seen this before,
So off he strode just missing a paw,
Now the cat got angry and the mouse was near,
But the rodent turned round and struck the cat with fear,
With eyes aflame and teeth blood-red,
Straight out the door and away the cat fled,
Now the mouse's problem was solved by a look,
But still the rain beat down into every cranny and nook.

Abigail Hilditch (11)
The Whartons Primary School

I Sit

I sit next to the window in school,
Just be calm and cool,
Don't be tempted to look out,
Keep down, don't shout.

I sit there fidgeting with my thumbs,
Trying to be calm, don't look dumb,
Throw a rubber,
In the gutter.

If I look, I'll get told off,
Don't make a sound not even a cough,
My eyes are stinging,
In my head I'm singing.

'Look out, look out,'
It shouts.
My fingers shaking,
But I'm not faking.

My eyes look,
I try to move them but they're stuck,
'Emma stand in front of the class!'
My eyes shoot away from the glass.

Emma Phimister (11)
The Whartons Primary School

Flowers

In spring the flowers start to grow,
Standing pretty in a row,
Daffodils yellow and pretty white,
Standing pretty what a lovely sight.

Katherine Quinn (7)
The Whartons Primary School

Playground Poem

One day I went to school,
There was a giant change,
Miles of banana trees,
With monkeys on the range.
All the way they scampered,
Dodging through the trees,
Jumping over hills of gold,
And running from the bees.
As they sat down with their friends,
Drinking coconut milk,
Fiddling with materials,
Oranges made from silk.
I thought they were mischievous,
I thought they were quite mean,
Then I seemed to notice,
I really was quite keen.
I started to join in, with their silly games,
Then I began to wonder,
If these things had names,
Then the day came to an end,
Sunset going down,
Soon the jungle faded,
I was down in town,
Whenever I go to school,
I always will watch out,
For all
    I know
        Monkeys are
            About.

Philip Britteon (10)
The Whartons Primary School

Untitled

Tall man
Little man
Big man
Small
Jade's jumping up
Pretending she is tall.

Four foot six,
Five foot one,
Seven foot three,
Two foot one.

Everyone is special,
In their own little way,
So if you think you're special,
Jump up and shout 'Hooray!'

Tall man,
Short man,
Big man,
Small,
Jade's jumping up
Pretending she is tall.

Jack Richings (10)
The Whartons Primary School

Winter's Coming

Outside the snow is falling,
Covering everything in sight,
The birds decide to take flight,
Up and up they fly,
The squirrel hides in the tree,
The rabbits are nowhere to be seen,
It's cold outside,
But I am sat by the fireside.

Jodie Swift (10)
The Whartons Primary School

The Seasons Order

Snow falls,
Bells call,
Bears hide,
We play with pride.

We build with snow
And this we know
This is winter's order.

Spring has a slight ping in its warmth,
The sprinklers are ready to sprinkle,
The bears are ready to eat with no sleep,
And this we know,
This is spring's order.

Summer, there's that slight murmur,
With . . . bees and birds and summery herbs,
When it's the end
When there's no bend . . .
And this we know,
This is summer's order.

Then there's autumn,
I know I have not written a lot
But if I did my brain would clot.

Bethan Grubb (9)
The Whartons Primary School

Colourful Jungle

Down in the jungle where it never ever snows,
Where the yellow monkey swings and the pink tree grows,
There's a little green croc drinking lemon iced tea,
Shouting out loud 'There's plenty more here for you and me.'

Sarah Campbell (10)
The Whartons Primary School

My Dog

My dog is cute,
He even wears a suit,
He always causes trouble,
And hates bubbles,
He loves his food,
But he's always rude,
He likes walking,
Also barking,
Well, what can I say?
That's my dog.

Kelly Thomas (10)
The Whartons Primary School

I Like Spring

I like spring because it's sunny,
And you may see a hopping bunny,
Lambs are bouncing here and there,
Trees are swaying in the air.

No more snow, no more gales,
Crocus growing over the dales,
Snowdrops blow in the breeze,
Time for those yummy cream teas.

Amy Wilson (10)
The Whartons Primary School

Playtime

At playtime there is shouting children,
Talking teachers, telling off teachers,
Children playing, children talking,
Whistles blowing, children stopping,
Lined up as quiet as a mouse,
That's not fair, it's the end of break.

Emma Hartley (7)
The Whartons Primary School

In My Pencil Case

I look inside my pencil case,
And what do I see?
I see a pretty rubber,
With a big bumblebee.
Underneath my rubber,
I see a yellow pin,
It's very, very shiny,
It has a picture of a hen,
I have many, many more things,
In my pencil case,
It has a picture of a shoe,
And a very long lace.

Rebecca Jane Thomas (8)
The Whartons Primary School

A Poem To Be Spoken Silently

It was so quiet that
I heard a centipede skid
Across the thundering floor.

It was so quiet that
I heard the sunlight shine
On the glittering glass.

It was so quiet that
I heard the frying pan sizzle
As I fried a shiny egg.

Olivia Coyle (8)
The Whartons Primary School

People

People are small,
People are big, some even act like a baby pig,
Some are fat, some are thin, some can't even
                                    see a thing,
Some are poorly, some dead, some you won't
                                    dare to dread!
Some are naughty, some are kind, some you
                                    can't even find.
Some like sports, some like books, some of
                            them have got good looks,
Some do all the housework and cook.

Daniel Atkinson (8)
The Whartons Primary School

Home Time

Home time is the best,
I see my dad or mum,
Also my teacher's say
I'm not too bad,
I go home with my mum and dad
And watch TV,
Sometimes I go to bed at ten to ten,
Stan goes to school with me,
Yes, school is over for the Christmas term
And also the clock strikes three!

Jordon Lawrence (7)
The Whartons Primary School

The Explorer's Attic

Up into a misty room,
Up,
    Up,
        Up,
Smells of trees burning in a forest,
Sounds of animals,
Louder and louder,
Thousands of antiques,
Cluttering the room up,
Loads of pictures and trophies,
You approach the end of the room,
Then you find a hidden door,
Rusty and broken,
The door handle is round and heavy,
You open it and find a cage,
Inside that cage there is a dragon,
Blocking the way through,
You squeeze through the gap,
And you find lots and lots
Of work on paper,
Making heaps and heaps on the table,
And on the chairs.
You find a bed and there is a man
Sleeping in it and accidentally you wake him,
Then you run away very quietly and escape.
Welcome to the explorer's attic!

Alex William Holmes (9)
Towngate Primary School

The Explorer's Attic

Up
   Up
      Up
In a dark, dark attic,
Lots of mice,
Creaking doors,
Slimy wall, flashing light,
Makes all things bright,
Up, up, up,
Higher you go glowing shadows,
Seeing ghosts, draughty windows
Under your feet,
Higher and higher
You never stop, you never reach
The top of the explorer's attic.

Joshua Ward (9)
Towngate Primary School

The Alien Spacecraft

Nine slimy steps going down
Down
Down
Blood on the walls,
A ceiling with holes in,
At the bottom, a door,
A door handle with spindles on,
Open the door,
Rats and bats,
Another door, dusty and old,
Open it,
There are aliens on this craft.

William Ward (9)
Towngate Primary School

The Inventor's Workshop

Slowly creeping curiously
Down
    Down,
        Down,
The stairs
Steam coming through the door,
Grab the door handle,
The doors are red as flames from a fire,
As I walk in, it's warm
Suspiciously stare all around the place,
See teddies that talk, electric pencils,
Roses hung on the ceiling top.
Welcome to the inventor's workshop.

Chloe Taylor (8)
Towngate Primary School

The Inventor's Workshop

Twelve sawdust stairs going
Down
    Down,
        Down,
            Down,
To the bottom,
You see the door,
Colourful as a rainbow,
The handle yellow as a daffodil
You go in,
Paint is everywhere,
Pots are drying,
Welcome to the inventor's workshop.

Conner Chappell (8)
Towngate Primary School

The Alien Spacecraft

In my garden a UFO appeared
I went to look closer
Some stairs shot out and made me jump,
I walked into the UFO
It was clean and smelt like oranges,
At the front, two purple aliens
Were messing with gadgets,
As quick as lightning I shot up,
      Up
            Up
Into orbit,
In the corner there were flags
And spacesuits,
I put on a suit and picked out
The English flag.
The UFO crash-landed on Mars
It was red as blood,
I leapt out and put the flag down,
I got back in the UFO
I flew home,
Thank you for riding the
Alien spacecraft.

Joe Batchelor (9)
Towngate Primary School

A Giant's Castle

One long path, too slimy to walk on,
Step, step, step,
Three steps go up diagonally,
Up,
    Up,
        Up,
I look through the giant keyhole,
It's a warm, cosy, delightful home,
It gives me a happy feeling,
I open the door using the rusty handle,
Inside I see the walls,
They are golden, they shine and
Shimmer in the sunlight,
I silently walk on the lovely floorboards,
They look like they have just been polished,
I now come to a white door,
I open it, daintily.
I gasp as I see silver walls glistening like a diamond sky,
I look up and gasp again,
A chandelier, it glitters beautifully,
I am in a giant's castle!

Kimberley Goulthorp (9)
Towngate Primary School

The Monster's Cave

Three stone steps going
Up,
   Up,
      Up,
Feel for a door, rough as an old oak tree trunk,
A large round room evolves from the darkness,
Go up some more steps this time
They're slimy,
There is a large leaking roof,
Cobwebs hang glistening on each rock,
It smells of old socks,
Large shadows dodge around like
Shadows of people dancing,
Strange plants sprout out of the walls,
There is an occasional bang,
Like someone dropping a tin,
Footsteps echo,
A pile of stones crack the ceiling,
Have you seen the monster's cave?

Toni Labourn (9)
Towngate Primary School

The Monster's Cave

In the middle of a
Mysterious forest
Was a pitch-black cave,
Was a grave
Blood and body pieces were on the floor,
No one wandering here heard of again,
Do not go because he is waiting,
Just waiting to get you,
The mysterious monster is waiting to eat you!

Thomas Kershaw (8)
Towngate Primary School

Monster's Cave

A dark open cave,
Shadows all over the place,
A spider dripping,
Down,
    Down,
        Down,
Smells like a stick of glue,
That has not got a lid,
Echoes of footsteps crushing
On bones and bones,
Approaching a door, red as demons,
Feel a handle rusty as leaves,
Push the door, hear the creak,
Shadows are coming,
Up,
    Up,
        Up,
In front of you a sign appears,
Welcome to the monster's cave!

Jordana Standage (9)
Towngate Primary School

The Witch's Kitchen

Going down a sticky corridor,
With your footsteps clapping on the floor,
You come to a rusty door,
It smells like old socks,
You try and feel where the door handle is,
All of the floor is dusty, dirty and smelly,
There is a broomstick in the corner,
Webs hang from the bumpy walls,
Frogs jump around you,
You are now in the witch's kitchen!

Kimara Parfitt (8)
Towngate Primary School

The Alien's Spacecraft

Up,
Up,
Up,
Climbing into the spacecraft,
When inside you can see lights
As bright as the sun,
You look at the door,
Blue as the shining sea,
Then you feel the controls,
Smooth as glimmering glass,
You enter the door,
Green aliens jump out at you,
I can see gamma rays firing lasers,
Welcome to the alien's spacecraft.

Thomas English (8)
Towngate Primary School

The Witches' Kitchen

I go up,
     Up,
          Up to the top of a mountain,
I find a door as rough as a tree trunk
I turn the handle as round as a ball,
There I find a kitchen as cold as ice,
The kitchen smells of old sweaty socks,
There in the corner, I see two scruffy broomsticks,
All of a sudden, I see a jar full of eyeballs
As slimy as goo,
I see a spider,
Witches shoot out on me,
Welcome to the witches' kitchen.

Emma Stoner (9)
Towngate Primary School

The Witch's Kitchen

100 sticky steps,
Sixty smelly stones,
Going
    Up,
            Up,
                  Up,
Mysterious moonbeams shine down on a shadowy castle,
It smells like burning glass and rubber,
Open the dusty door,
A crackling cauldron meets you,
Sounds like dry leaves being crushed,
Jinxed jellies jump,
Popping potions pounce,
Self-peeling potatoes plop into a pot,
Welcome to the witch's kitchen.

Charlotte Auty (8)
Towngate Primary School

The Explorer's Attic

Ten creaking steps,
Going up,
        Up,
           Up,
Then came a rusty door,
A burning smell of rubber,
Echoes of people chatting round the corner,
Coming nearer and nearer,
Feel the handle, cold and rough,
You open the dusty door,
Come inside, you see heaps of treasure,
Books fill the room,
Old walking boots everywhere,
Welcome to the explorer's attic.

Daniel Stephenson (8)
Towngate Primary School

The Inventor's Workshop

A grotty old workshop,
With a grotty old handle,
A man worked all night,
Clay splattered everywhere,
Statues drying,
Pottery machines,
Broken statues ready to be fixed,
Books full of pictures,
Good and exciting ideas for more
And more brand new statues,
The man who works here wears
A mucky old apron,
If you went inside
You would say it's a tip,
Dust everywhere,
Clay everywhere,
It will make you sneeze,
Welcome to the inventor's workshop.

Tom Pitchforth (8)
Towngate Primary School

The Inventor's Workshop

One large wet step
Rusty round door handle,
Squeaky creaky door open
Inside it smells of cleaning polish,
It is warm and cosy like
Sitting in a fire,
Approaching a big table with robots' bodies,
Lying ready to be fixed,
Everywhere things are scattered,
Floorboards squeaking like a cat miaowing,
Full of bright colours, red, blue, green.
A robot's voice getting nearer and nearer,
Welcome to the inventor's workshop.

Philippa Bayford (9)
Towngate Primary School

The Monster's Cave

In the creepy cave
Further,
Further,
And further,
You go into the cave
It smells of rotten cheese
You can hear wet and slimy drips
Dripping from the ceiling
Down,
Down,
    Down,
I come to a door,
As gold as the sun
A rusty old handle,
I turn it with a giant squeal
The door opens,
What do I see?
Broken chains from the treasure chest,
I hear shouting in the background,
No one who enters is never heard of again,
Welcome to the monster's cave!

Kirsty Scott (8)
Towngate Primary School

The Witch's Kitchen

Go up to the dusty, dirty door,
Open the creaky door very slowly,
There are three stone steps going down
    Down,
        Down,
The floor is like a sticky lollipop,
A wicked laugh is getting nearer and nearer,
Red worktops, red as blood,
It is very dark, dark as the night,
Creaking floorboards like a squeaking mouse,
A dirty sink, dirty as soil,
Loud footsteps getting closer and closer.
Broomsticks in every corner,
Welcome to the witch's kitchen.

Toni-Lee Edwards (9)
Towngate Primary School

The Alien Spacecraft

Controls litter the labs of doom,
Aliens await you in the next room,
Holes lead to alien beds,
Sleeping carpets lie over toxic blegs,
Space guns shoot on booby traps,
Robots clank and smash round the craft,
Hey, guess where you are now?
Falling down,
    Down,
        Down,
An escalator next to an escape rope,
Welcome to the alien spacecraft.
Watch the beams!

Joshua Leach (8)
Towngate Primary School

Monster's Bath

Nine quiet steps slipping,
Down,
Down,
Down,
Smells of a brown burning stick in the fireplace,
Nearer and nearer,
Appearing, a old, splintered, monstery wand,
Appearing, a dirty, rusty, old, rough door,
The door in front is a spider's tunnel,
At the end of the tunnel is a big,
Brown, smooth door, cobra's coil under your feet,
Inside the room, is a mysterious green slide
It leads into a big pool of beans,
Welcome to the monster's bath.

Aaron Peters (8)
Towngate Primary School

The Witch's Kitchen

A dark stairway winding
Down
    Down,
Smells like the smell of a bubbling
Poison potion,
Down one step,
Down two steps,
Until all eight steps are done,
Voices growl behind the ancient door,
Spiders scuttle,
Cobra's slither out of the gloom,
Reach for the cobweb-covered door,
Suddenly a panther jumps from above,
It is blocking the way.

Annie Peake (8)
Towngate Primary School

The Witch's Kitchen

    Up,
        Up,
            Up,
The smelly, dangerous stairs,
Leading to the self-centred witch,
She'll grind your bones,
Never dare, never dare,
If you care about your bones.

The smell is yet so firm and dead,
She'll kill, she'll kill, dead, dead, dead,
Approaching a rusty door to the
Courageous killing, low life witch,
'To the kitchen' she said,
Down, down, down, went pots and pans,
Who knows, who knows what she will do.
'Argh!'

Aimee Louise Kershaw (9)
Towngate Primary School

The Explorer's Attic

Going up the stairs,
  1,
    2,
      3,
        4,
The walls golden as the sun,
Smells like violets and roses,
Pots and pans, pens on the stairs,
Finally reach the door,
Colourful like a rainbow,
Reach out to open the door,
The handle is round and red,
Come inside you can hardly walk,
Treasure, hats, books and all sorts,
Welcome to the explorer's attic.

Caroline Lewis (8)
Towngate Primary School

The Inventor's Workshop

The inventor's workshop is big
Full of machines and broken toys
There is nowhere to walk
Except for the way to a giant door,
When you open the door
You go up,
    Up,
        Up,
            Up,
Until you reach the top,
Then you reach a cupboard,
Inside the cupboard there are old boxes,
Full to the top with parts of machines,
Behind the boxes the inventor's making toys.

Welcome to the inventor's workshop.

Harry English (8)
Towngate Primary School

The Witch's Kitchen

Going up to the old rusty door,
Up,
    Up,
        Up,
            Up,
Over the stony path,
Where some blood hangs from the ceiling,
Got to the old smelly rusty door,
With half a cracked handle,
Open the door,
Shut your eyes and open them,
Look around you, argh!
Uhh look snakes slithering
Cats miaowing.
Welcome to the witch's kitchen.

Amelia Ann Clayton (9)
Towngate Primary School

The Witch's Kitchen

Five concrete steps large and hard
You go up one then another and another up
One and land on the last one,
You open the creaking door,
A large shadow walks out of the kitchen,
You find a room, open it and there stands
A room full of dusty, smelly and broken
Witch's brooms.
You slam the door shut,
You look on the kitchen table
And see a cooked frog,
On the floor slugs and snails
Across leaving shiny silver trails,
You can hear footsteps coming from the stairs,
There stands a large, ugly, smelly witch,
Welcome to the witch's kitchen.

Richard Athorne (8)
Towngate Primary School

The Explorer's Attic

Fifteen creaky steps climbing
Up,
   Up,
      Up,
Into the old, rotten attic,
The explorer would rather keep the attic filled
With old ripped games, boxes, chairs and tables,
It is very, very dusty and messy,
I wouldn't dare go up,
It is gloomy,
You walk into lots of things,
You would hurt yourself,
It's very messy,
Welcome to the explorer's attic.

Charley Sheard (8)
Towngate Primary School

The Witch's Kitchen

Five steps to the kitchen
One, two,
Three, four,
Five,
Poison ivy drooping on the walls,
Red and cream cupboards,
Bats swinging from beam to beam,
Black cat sits on the broomstick,
The windows have streaks of blood
Coming down them,
Creaking cupboard doors,
Like a croaking frog,
Cauldron full of bats, frogs and spiders,
Potion books all over, poisons in bottles,
Suddenly the witch creeps up on you,
She has green hair,
A net over her head,
Purple hat with green ribbon round it,
Chopping knives all over the place,
The cat knocks the broomstick over,
The broomstick knocks the witch out,
Snakes surround you,
You're standing on pins, sharp as crocodiles' teeth,
Welcome to the witch's kitchen,
'Aarrgghh!'

Blythe Senior (8)
Towngate Primary School